SOUTHWEST CANYON COUNTRY'S BEST NATURE WALKS

SOUTHWEST CANYON COUNTRY'S BEST NATURE WALKS

39 EASY WAYS TO EXPLORE THE NATIONAL PARKS OF THE FOUR CORNERS

RODDY SCHEER

TIMBER PRESS + PORTLAND, OREGON

To Edward Abbey and Stewart Udall for helping us love and cherish Southwest canyon country

Frontispiece: Devil's Garden Trail, Arches National Park
Opposite: Cliff Palace, Mesa Verde National Park

Timber Press
Workman Publishing
Hachette Book Group, Inc.
1290 Avenue of the Americas
New York, NY 10104
timberpress.com

Timber Press is an imprint of Workman Publishing, a division of Hachette Book Group, Inc. The Timber Press name and logo are registered trademarks of Hachette Book Group, Inc.

Printed in China on responsibly sourced paper.

Jacket and text design by Sarah Crumb,
based on a series design by Hillary Caudle

The publisher is not responsible for websites (or their content) that are not owned by the publisher.

The Hachette Speakers Bureau provides a wide range of authors for speaking events. To find out more, go to hachettespeakersbureau.com or email hachettespeakers@hbgusa.com.

ISBN 978-1-64326-323-6

A catalog record for this book is available from the Library of Congress.

CONTENTS

INTRODUCTION

In the vast expanse of the American Southwest lies a landscape that defies comprehension—a realm of sculpted stone, labyrinthine canyons, and an ever-changing palette of colors that dance with the shifting sunlight. Here, in the heart of canyon country, nature reveals itself in its most striking and mesmerizing forms. It's a place where every step tells a story, where the whispers of ancient civilizations echo through the wind, and where the raw beauty of the Earth is on full display.

Southwest Canyon Country's Best Nature Walks invites you to embark on a journey through this enchanting realm, offering a curated selection of short nature hikes that reveal the splendor and secrets of the American Southwest. From the towering cliffs of Zion to the cliff dwellings of Mesa Verde, each trail beckons with the promise of adventure and discovery.

But these are not the epic treks of seasoned adventurers or the grueling expeditions of intrepid explorers. Instead, these are gentle strolls—brief excursions that can be enjoyed by families, solo travelers, and nature enthusiasts of all ages and abilities. Whether you're seeking a peaceful retreat into the wilderness or simply craving a breath of fresh air, *Southwest Canyon Country's Best Nature Walks* has something for everyone.

▲ The Painted Wall, Black Canyon of the Gunnison National Park

Within these pages, you'll find detailed descriptions of each hike, complete with difficulty ratings and insider tips to enhance your experience. But this is more than just a guidebook—it's a celebration of the profound connection between humanity and the natural world. It's a reminder that, even in our modern age of technology and urban sprawl, there are still places where the wild spirit of the Earth reigns supreme. It's an invitation to slow down, to breathe deeply, and to savor the simple pleasures of a leisurely walk in the great outdoors. So lace up your boots, pack a water bottle and a camera, and prepare to embark on an unforgettable odyssey through the canyon country of the American Southwest.

UTAH

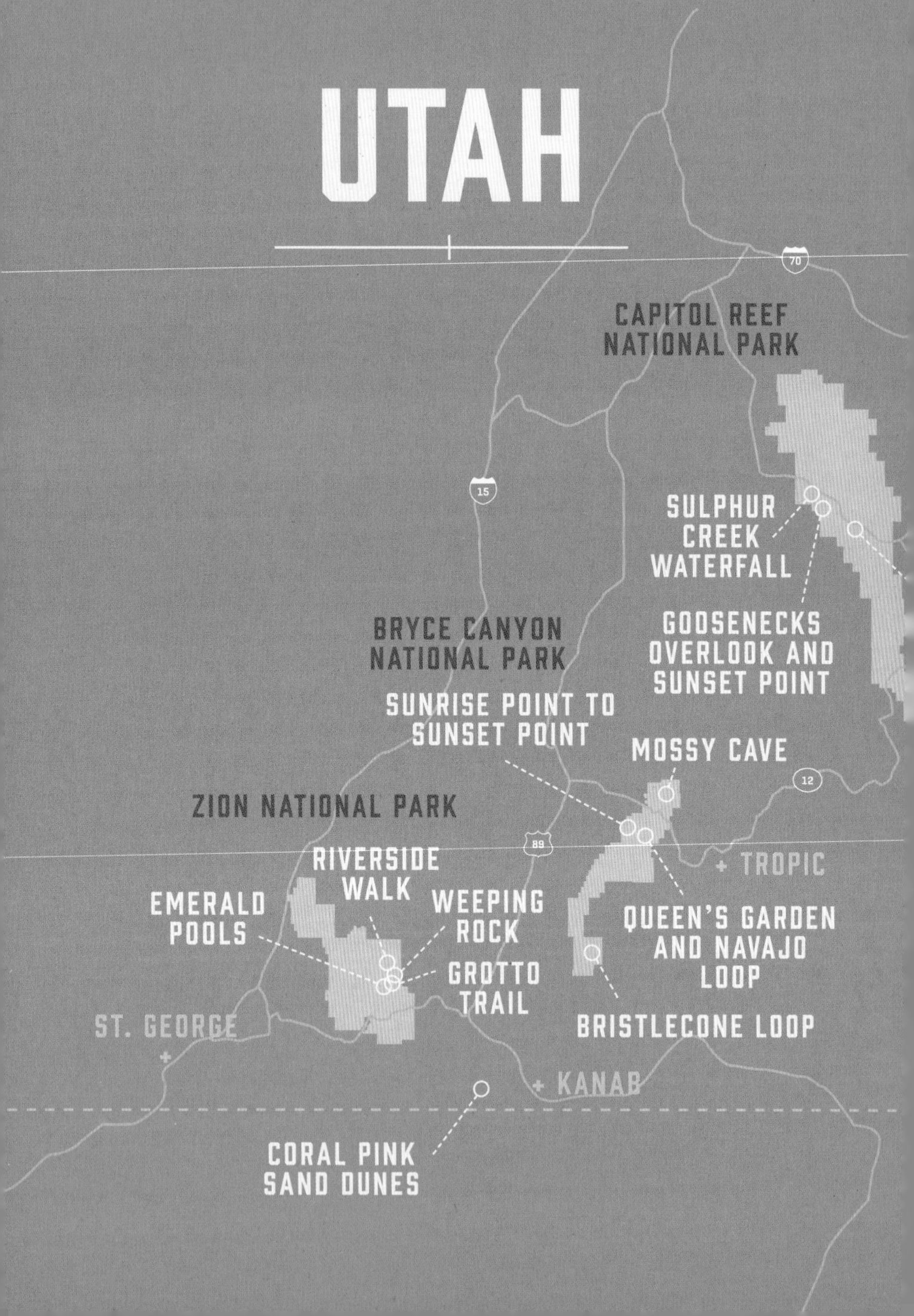

70

CAPITOL REEF NATIONAL PARK

15

SULPHUR CREEK WATERFALL

GOOSENECKS OVERLOOK AND SUNSET POINT

BRYCE CANYON NATIONAL PARK

SUNRISE POINT TO SUNSET POINT

MOSSY CAVE

12

ZION NATIONAL PARK

89

TROPIC

RIVERSIDE WALK

EMERALD POOLS

WEEPING ROCK

GROTTO TRAIL

QUEEN'S GARDEN AND NAVAJO LOOP

ST. GEORGE

BRISTLECONE LOOP

KANAB

CORAL PINK SAND DUNES

ARCHES NATIONAL PARK

LANDSCAPE ARCH

DELICATE ARCH

PARK AVENUE

THE WINDOWS AND DOUBLE ARCH

70

191

313

24

MOAB

RUITA

UPHEAVAL DOME

MESA ARCH

GRAND VIEW POINT

GRAND WASH

MONTICELLO

CANYONLANDS NATIONAL PARK

191

COLORADO

UTAH

ARIZONA

ARCHES NATIONAL PARK

PARK AVENUE

Explore this wide desert valley between 600-foot-tall Entrada sandstone monoliths

DIFFICULTY
Easy

LOCATION
Courthouse Towers, southwest Arches

LENGTH
2 miles

WHEELCHAIR ACCESSIBLE
Partially, the first 250 feet to viewpoint

PETS ALLOWED
No

Take a stroll down Park Avenue—Arches style! Here, instead of tall buildings lining an urban midtown motorway, you'll experience a 2-mile out-and-back hiking trail featuring a wide range of desert flora and flanked by massive 600-plus-foot-tall Entrada sandstone cliffs capped with jagged tops.

To get there from the Arches National Park Entrance Station (5 miles north of Moab, Utah), drive 2.3 miles on Arches National Park Road to the well-marked Park Avenue parking area on the left (north) side of the road. If all the spots are full, wait a few minutes as most visitors just check out the overlook and then drive on.

Park and make your way on foot north on the paved path for another 250 feet to the Park Avenue Viewpoint. Looking down into the valley between monolithic rock walls that slightly resemble the New York City skyline, it's easy to see why early white settlers named this spot after Manhattan's Park Avenue, the posh New York City thoroughfare lined with similarly monolithic but man-made buildings and mansions.

◂ Looking out from the Park Avenue Viewpoint provides a good overview of the geological forces at work at Arches National Park.

Utah's Park Avenue is the first major rock formation most of us will see upon visiting Arches, given its proximity to the park entrance. And the view here provides a great introduction to how the unique rock formations of Arches came to be.

▾ Western aster lends a pop of color to Park Avenue's otherwise red rock and green landscape.

Four Jurassic-period strata make up the different iconic rock formations found in today's national park. The oldest, Navajo sandstone, was deposited some 200 million years ago as a massive dune field, stretching 7 miles northeast from around the modern-day location of the park visitor center and terminating beyond the Windows arches. You are actually walking right on this oldest stratum as you traverse the lower stretches of the trail through Park Avenue as it gets closer to Courthouse Towers.

Then, approximately 160 million years ago, ancient tidal flats from what

◂ Dwarf lupine can tolerate the poor desert soils of southeastern Utah.

was then an ocean shoreline covered the region here in sediment that over time *lithified* (or turned to rock) into what geologists now call the Dewey Bridge Member. These days you can see the Dewey Bridge stratum, with its chocolate-brown and wavy-lined appearance due to irregular erosion patterns, underneath just about every major rock formation and arch within the national park. Indeed, this muddy sandstone layer erodes much more quickly than the Entrada sandstone that sits on it, sometimes leading to top-heavy "mushroom" rocks, like at nearby Balanced Rock.

Cut to 140 million years ago, and the "slickrock" Entrada sandstone entered the scene as coastal dunes that eventually lithified into the stratum that these days plays host to just about all of the iconic formations of Arches National Park. This rock layer is prone to vertical fracturing and joint weathering—when water seeps into fractures, dissolving the calcite cement bonding the sandstone together. Look for the rounded slabs of rock missing from the walls of the various skyscrapers of Park Avenue to see future arches already starting to form.

Lichens—like these Acarosporaceae—are dual life-forms consisting of an algae and a fungus working together so both species' needs are met. ▾

Keep walking as the trail beyond the viewpoint turns to dirt and commences down a series of stairsteps that trailmakers constructed into the hillside to help hikers down the steepest part of the hike. You'll lose about 100 feet in elevation just over 0.1 mile.

From left: A common side-blotched lizard tries to sneak up a rock face.

Eaton's penstemon

At the bottom of the stairsteps, the trail becomes more *suggested* than well-defined. Occasional rock cairns help guide you along, as well as others' footsteps in the sand at low spots in the rocky substrate you are now hiking across. Pick your way forward, staying in the middle of the "avenue," and you won't get lost. Swirly patterns in the slickrock sandstone on the canyon floor here show where different layers of sand and sediment were sculpted by ancient floodwater inundations and other erosional assaults.

While plants are few and far between here in the desert, an occasional Utah juniper tree grows twisty and stunted. Although these trees aren't much taller than a human, some of them are upwards of 600 years old. They are able to survive by sending down a deep taproot that can access underground aquifers deeper than neighboring plants can reach. A host of other lower growing plants—desert prince's plume, blackbrush, common peppergrass, yellow rabbitbrush, green ephedra, Harriman's yucca, and Sonoran scrub oak, among others—dot the otherwise red rock landscape in green. Meanwhile, dozens of wildflower species—dwarf lupine, rough mule's ears, stemless four-nerved daisy, Eaton's penstemon, Utah daisy, and desert paintbrush, to name a few—bloom in spring and summer.

Regarding wildlife, desert animals tend to be crepuscular—they come out at the edges of the day and/or at night when temperatures aren't as high and the sand isn't as hot. One such nocturnal forager here that's uniquely adapted to life in the desert is the kangaroo rat, one of nineteen rodent

species calling Arches home. These small, long-tailed mouse lookalikes—named for the way they hop around using just their two hind legs like kangaroos—consume *only* plant matter, deriving all the water they need to survive from the seeds, beans, and nuts they eat. They can store dozens of seeds at once in their fur-lined cheek pouches while transporting them to favorite caching spots.

Meanwhile, mule deer, porcupines, red foxes, coyotes, mountain lions, skunks, ringtails, and bobcats also tend to follow a crepuscular regimen. While you are less than likely to see any of these animals unless you are camping in the park and you get lucky, chances are good you will see or hear one or more bird species.

Ravens, which are closely related to crows, make themselves at home here, while songbirds like the house finch and evening grosbeak are also quite common. Raptors of all kinds also like it around here, given all the great perching spots. To wit, peregrine falcons can sometimes be seen patrolling the skies above Park Avenue in search of their favorite food, songbirds. Arguably the fastest animal on the planet, a peregrine can reach speeds of 240 miles per hour when diving to knock out another bird it's targeted as prey. It then scoops up the dead bird and eats it.

These speedy raptors can be found on six continents, but they are a lot less common than they used to be before the widespread application of the synthetic pesticide DDT from the late 1940s until the 1970s. Populations of peregrine falcons, bald eagles, and lots of other birds declined rapidly. It wasn't until Rachel Carson sounded the alarm about DDT in her 1962 book *Silent Spring* that activists and government agencies started working in concert to eliminate this major

Above, from left: Look for interesting wave patterns in the Navajo sandstone you are hiking across at Park Avenue. These patterns were created by overlapping sediment deposits some 200 million years ago.

An opportunistic blackbrush plant grows out of a small crack in the sandstone.

threat to wildlife and ecosystems. The eventual banning of DDT and endangered species protection helped bring peregrines back from the brink of extinction. The bird was removed from the U.S. endangered species list in 1999, but is still considered endangered by the state of Utah.

After a mile, you'll get to the end of the "avenue" where the skyscrapers no longer stand. Courthouse Towers, another monolithic cliff face, is to your right about 700 feet away, while the triple-headed formation called the Three Gossips is approximately 900 feet due west. You'll be at the low point of the hike, 300 feet in elevation below the trailhead. (If the trail dumps you out onto the Park Road, you've gone too far.)

Take a drink, eat a snack, and turn around, following the Navajo sandstone "trail" back the way you came. Enjoy the opposite perspective on the skyscraper formations alongside Park Avenue as you hike back, with later light hitting the rocks at different angles than when you came down earlier. You may even see some wildflowers and rock patterns along the trail that you missed on the way in.

Now that you've seen Park Avenue and have a bit of understanding about what makes Arches tick geologically and ecologically, it's time to move deeper into the national park and see some of the other interesting ways Mother Nature has sculpted out this red rock sandstone domain.

Hikers at the end of the Park Avenue Trail get great views of the Three Gossips and Courthouse Towers. ▾

ARCHES NATIONAL PARK

THE WINDOWS AND DOUBLE ARCH

One short hike plus five arches equals wow!

	DIFFICULTY Easy
LOCATION The Windows, southeastern Arches	LENGTH 1.8 miles
WHEELCHAIR-ACCESSIBLE Partially, with paved path to Double Arch Trail, but sandy at end	PETS ALLOWED No

The Windows section of Arches is backed up by the snow-capped peaks of the La Sal Mountains.

While some of the arches here at Arches National Park can be seen from behind the windshield, there's nothing like getting out on foot and exploring them up close in the context of the local landscape and ecosystem. Perhaps nowhere in the park is this easier to accomplish than at the Windows, where you can visit Turret Arch, the North and South Windows, the Parade of Elephants, and the tallest arch in the park, Double Arch, in less than an hour over the course of an easy 1.8-mile loop hike.

To get there from the Arches National Park Entrance Station (5 miles north of the city of Moab, Utah), drive 9.2 miles on Arches National Park Road and then turn right (just past Balanced Rock) onto the Windows Road, which dead-ends at a circular parking area 2.5 miles to the east. Park at the Windows Section parking area—the first one you'll come to on the one-way parking loop—and look for the well-marked trailhead for the Windows.

Balanced Rock, seen here with a starvation prickly pear cactus bloom in the foreground, is near the junction to the turnoff for the Windows Section. ▾

Follow the paved trail for about a quarter mile and take the spur trail off to the right for 0.1 mile as it climbs up underneath the dramatic 65-foot-high span of Turret Arch, which is in turn dwarfed by a much larger turret-shaped rock tower right next to it that may erode out into another Balanced Rock at some point in the future. Several smaller "mushroom rock" turrets are on the

▲ Twolobe larkspur guides the way up to Turret Arch and its surrounding towers.

opposite side of the arch emanating from the same Entrada sandstone base.

Blackbrush, a low-lying twiggy perennial shrub adapted to life with little water, dominates the floral realm around here. This aromatic dark green shrub with short, rigid branches that taper to a sharp point likes to prevail over the landscape where it can, usually in stretches of sandy, well-drained soil like here around Turret Arch and throughout Arches National Park. This tough cookie of a plant only produces fruit and seeds in abundant precipitation years, and generally goes dormant every summer, when temperatures here frequently top 95°F. Small mammals and birds consume the plant's seeds. In winter when the pickings are thin, mule deer and bighorn sheep browse blackbrush's little leaves and nibble on its branches to eke out what nutrition they can.

Of course, other plants pick their spots between the seemingly ubiquitous blackbrush. There seems to be at least one Utah juniper tree, living or dead, in every picture taken at and around Arches. Just because these twisted-trunk trees don't get much taller than you and me doesn't mean they are short-lived. In fact, many of them live past their 600th birthdays. Once they do die, their reaching, contorted trunks often remain in place for decades if not

▲ Starvation prickly pear cacti send out colorful blooms in spring.

longer, becoming permanent fixtures in the desert landscape and providing habitat for all kinds of rodents, reptiles, and insects. Twolobe larkspur, narrowleaf yucca, bottlebrush squirreltail, bitterbrush, blue grama, big sagebrush, lobeleaf grounsel, Gambel oak, and desert globemallow are among the other usual suspects filling in various gaps on the sandy desert floor.

After you've explored around and underneath Turret Arch, hike back down the 0.1-mile spur trail and continue on the loop toward the Windows, which you'll see directly ahead of you. In another 0.1 mile go left at the fork and follow the trail right up to North Window Arch, which is 93 feet wide by 51 feet tall. You can venture off the pavement and explore within and underneath the arch itself, from where you'll have great views back toward Turret Arch and the surrounding desert landscape. Chances are good you won't get the North Window to yourself; it's one of the most visited arches in the park and can feel a little crowded at times.

When you've had your fill of this pleasant midarch North Window perch, retrace your steps back to the previous trail junction and head south past the band of rock called the

Hikers in South Window Arch

▲ The Entrada sandstone rock named Nose Bridge separates the North Window and South Window arches.

Nose Bridge—it looks like a nose between the two "eyes" of the Windows arches—for another 0.1 mile to a viewpoint of the South Window, where the paved trail ends. Here you can go off the pavement as well and explore underneath the arch, although it is more difficult to access than its neighboring arch to the north. Measuring 105 feet wide by 65 feet high, South Window is the third largest arch in the park.

While you could turn around here and head back to your car via the paved trail you just traversed, a better idea for those unfazed by a little off-pavement terrain is to complete the loop via the "primitive trail" that runs around the south end of the Windows fin and then circles north with views into the less-visited east side of the formation. In the early morning this side of the Windows is often lit up in low-angled golden light. Although the trail is primitive, just about anyone can handle it. Best of all, you'll leave the crowds behind on the west side of the formation. Pinyon pines, Utah junipers, greasewood, and green ephedra vie for desert floor real estate. To the south and east, canyons cut by the Colorado River and Salt Creek winnow through a tormented landscape. Looking southeast, you can't miss the craggy,

Clockwise from top left: Pale evening primrose, desert paintbrush, prairie sunflower, and twolobe larkspur are just a few of the wildflower blooms adorning the desert in springtime around the Windows Section of Arches National Park.

snow-capped La Sal Mountains, with a dozen of the peaks topping 12,000 feet in elevation, just 20 miles away.

The primitive trail winds around the northern edge of the Windows fin, curving west after another half a mile of walking. Keep hiking over a sandstone bench—where you'll cross the fin—and within another 0.2 mile you'll be back at the parking lot.

But that's not all! You may as well continue on foot to check out the Parade of Elephants, an Entrada sandstone sculptural element carved by Mother Nature herself, and Double Arch, the tallest arch in the park and a feat of prehistoric erosional architecture; they are only a short 0.3-mile walk from here. Make your way across the middle of the parking loop via the Windows Connector Trail to the north side, where you will pick up the well-marked Double Arch Trail.

The trail to Double Arch is paved for the first 0.2 mile as it passes the Parade of Elephants, a series of overlapping Entrada sandstone cliffs that look like (you guessed it) a group of elephants on the savannah. Peer into the sandstone cliffs of this parade to find a small arch deep within.

Keep moving and in another 0.1 mile you'll be at Double Arch, which looks a little like a giant gyroscope embedded in red rock sandstone. The two overlapping arches that make up Double Arch share the same foundation stone. This formation is an excellent example of a "pothole" arch, formed when water collects in a natural depression and then chemical weathering from the buildup of calcium carbonate cuts through to form an opening. The trail, now sand and dirt, passes directly underneath the bigger of the two, which measures 144 feet wide by 112 feet tall. These dimensions qualify Double Arch as the tallest and the third widest or longest in the park.

Opposite, clockwise from top: The sun sets behind the Parade of Elephants, lighting up the desert in low-angled golden light.

The two arches of Double Arch share the same foundation.

A digger bee alights on a starvation prickly pear cactus bloom. Let the pollination begin!

The orange blooms of desert globemallow decorate the trailside near the Parade of Elephants. ▾

Enjoy the scenery and then retrace your steps back past the Parade of Elephants to the parking loop—you can hike the connector trail back to your car on the south side of that loop. You may not want to go, but when you do drive away, you'll no doubt leave this all-natural sculpture park possessing a newfound appreciation for the artistic skills of Mother Nature.

ARCHES NATIONAL PARK

DELICATE ARCH

You've seen it on the license plates, now visit the iconic arch of the Southwest in real life

DIFFICULTY
Easy

LOCATION
Delicate Arch Road, east-central Arches

LENGTH
300 ft. to 3 mi.

WHEELCHAIR ACCESSIBLE
Yes, to lower viewpoint only

PETS ALLOWED
No

Of the more than 2000 arches in Arches National Park, none is so famous as Delicate Arch. This icon of Southwest canyon country and the symbol of the state of Utah, freestanding and solitary on the edge of a rounded Entrada sandstone cliff, is a must-see for many visitors.

Delicate Arch is the largest freestanding arch in the park—it's not connected to any adjacent rock walls or fins—at 46 feet high by 32 feet wide, but you can't see it from the park road. The easiest way to see it for yourself would be to drive to the Lower Delicate Arch Viewpoint. To get there from the Arches National Park Entrance Station (5 miles north of the city of Moab, Utah), drive 11.7 miles on Arches National Park Road and turn right (east) onto Delicate Arch Road, which leads east for 2.3 more miles and dead-ends at a parking loop. Park the car and follow the well-marked paved path east just 300 feet to Lower Delicate Arch Viewpoint, from which you can see Delicate Arch perched on a distant cliff.

For an even better view, fork left on the viewpoint trail and hike the moderately challenging half mile (out-and-back) trail up to the Upper Delicate Arch Viewpoint, which gets you up higher and within a mile of Delicate Arch across a scenic red rock canyon.

There's no way to hike from either viewpoint directly to Delicate Arch, but if you are willing to do a bit of hiking across the desert—3 miles out and back with 470 feet of elevation gain, to be exact—drive back the way you came for 1.2 miles on Delicate Arch Road to the Delicate Arch Trailhead. Park there and pick up the trail near the bathrooms on the east side of the parking lot. Start hiking east and within 375 feet you'll pass Wolfe Ranch and its crude one-room cabin where John Wolfe homesteaded and raised cattle in the early 1900s.

At about 0.1 mile, fork left and follow this side trail for another 0.1 mile to see Ute petroglyphs dating back approximately 300 years depicting a stylized horse and rider

◂ Delicate Arch in the golden light of late afternoon

▲ The Ute petroglyphs off the Delicate Arch Trail are amazingly well-preserved given how old they are.

surrounded by bighorn sheep and doglike animals carved into an Entrada red rock sandstone cliff wall.

Continue forward on this side loop, which soon rejoins the main Delicate Arch Trail and begins to climb gradually over smooth slickrock sandstone. Make sure you have sturdy footwear with good traction, especially if there's any chance of rain.

At about a mile in, traverse a particularly challenging stretch of trail punctuated by large rocks and large sand deposits that make for slow going. Keep moving and soon enough the trail leads you up and over a rocky wall where you will be greeted with the jaw-dropping close-up view of Delicate Arch backed by the snow-capped La Sal Mountains some 20-plus miles in the distance to the southeast.

Pick a spot in the natural rock bowl that surrounds Delicate Arch and eat a snack, swig some water, and drink in the view. You can always join the queue for selfies at the arch, but don't expect to get the place to yourself. When you've had enough of Delicate Arch, turn around and retrace your steps for 1.5 miles back to the trailhead and parking lot, complete with the world's most famous arch checked off your bucket list.

ARCHES NATIONAL PARK

LANDSCAPE ARCH

The quintessential hike through this park, from Devil's Garden to Landscape Arch and beyond

DIFFICULTY
Easy

LOCATION
Devil's Garden, northwest Arches

LENGTH
1.8 to 4.7 miles

WHEELCHAIR ACCESSIBLE
No

PETS ALLOWED
No

The 1.8-mile out-and-back hike to Landscape Arch is an easy and scenic adventure that leads between tall sandstone fins and through quintessential southeastern Utah desert terrain to the widest of all the arches in Arches National Park.

To get there from the Arches National Park Entrance Station (5 miles north of the city of Moab, Utah), drive 17.3 miles on Arches National Park Road until it forks right into the one way parking loop at Devil's Garden, the northernmost section of Arches National Park. Follow this loop for another half mile and pull over in one of the parking spots along the right side of the road as close as you can get to the well-marked Devil's Garden trailhead (near the two bathrooms). The hike is flat and easy but you will traverse sandy, rocky terrain, so wear sturdy boots or hiking sneakers.

Start out on the wide and fairly level gravel-and-sand trail as it cuts northwest between Entrada sandstone fins that rise upwards of 60 feet on both sides of you. These very fins may someday host new arches as the forces of erosion and gravity work their magic on the sandstone.

Just 0.2 mile into the hike, choose whether to take the optional spur trail to the east (right) that leads to Tunnel Arch and Pine Tree Arch. Detouring on this Y-shaped out-and-back spur will add a half mile to your total hiking distance, but is well worth it if you're feeling spry and want to check as many arches off your list as you can. If you take the detour, go right at the Y for Tunnel Arch, which stands 25.5 feet wide and 14 feet high and is eroded entirely out of a massive 14-foot-wide sandstone wall. The circular shape of the arch and the fact that it cuts through such a thick wall make it look like a remnant section of a subway tunnel. Left at the Y leads to Pine Tree Arch, 46 feet wide by 48 feet high, so named for the pinyon pine trees that grace its opening and the surrounding area. While these pines may not look very old, don't be fooled by their diminutive height. Most of them around here are only 10 to 20 feet tall, but they can live upwards of 1000 years!

Of course, pinyon pines aren't the only flora thriving back here in the Devil's Garden. While Arches National Park only gets 8 to 10 inches of rain in a typical year, you wouldn't know it given how much greenery springs up trailside and as far as the eye can see. Within any given 10 feet of hiking, you might encounter sand sagebrush, narrowleaf yucca, hispid goldenaster, Navajo fleabane, starvation

▲ Hikers make their way along the Devil's Garden Trail.

Opposite, clockwise from top: The Fiery Furnace is a jumbled collection of sandstone canyons, fins, and arches that you can see off to the east as you make your way toward the Devil's Garden.

Sand sagebrush, recognizable by its wispy white stems, helps prevent erosion on sandy slopes.

The unique leaves of the sacred datura plant contain toxic alkaloids that keep wildlife from chewing on them.

Hispid goldenaster pops out of the unlikeliest cracks in the sandstone.

prickly pear cactus, and sacred datura. Both living and dead Utah juniper trees form curvy frames around many scenic views all along the hike.

If you stay still awhile and keep an eye on an old juniper trunk, you may just see some wildlife—a desert cottontail, a kangaroo rat, a western collared lizard, or a gopher snake—come out of hiding, thinking the coast is clear. Chances are you won't encounter one of Arches' midget faded rattlesnakes, a small subspecies of the western rattlesnake, as they are mostly active at night. Watch your step nevertheless, especially in the rock crevices where they sometimes roost, as their venom is extremely toxic. Rest assured only about a third of all rattlesnake bites contain enough venom

to hurt you. (If you do get bitten by a rattlesnake, call 911 and get medical aid within 30 minutes as the venom can do serious damage to bodily organs if left untreated.)

With that sobering advice in mind, gingerly make your way back to the main trail and head right (north), following the easy grade as it heads northwest. At 0.8 mile ignore the turnoff to the right (east) for the Primitive Trail—you will explore that on the way back if you extend the hike to Double O Arch—and start looking for Landscape Arch up and to the left (west). In another 0.1 mile you'll reach the overlook spot with the best view of the park's widest arch.

Indeed, the slender and graceful 77-foot-high Landscape Arch stretches 290 feet across, yet is only 6 feet thick at its

Clockwise, from above: Hikers on top of Double O Arch enjoy some of the best views of Arches National Park.

The dusky pink bloom of a starvation prickly pear cactus lends a pop of color to the otherwise red rock and green landscape.

Landscape Arch under the moon and stars

center. Its center was around 5 feet thicker until September 1, 1991, when hidden fractures in the rock precipitated loud cracking and popping noises before rock slabs, some as big as 60 feet long, fell from the arch's thinnest underside section. No one was hurt, but the deposition of some 180 tons of fresh rock debris directly below the arch convinced the National Park Service to disallow hikers beneath Landscape Arch ever since, given the safety risk.

While Landscape Arch may be the star attraction here, don't miss Partition Arch, where Mother Nature seems to have constructed a rock partition down the middle of the arch, high on the same sandstone fin to the right (northwest).

Part of the Primitive Trail takes hikers up and along the top of a sandstone fin some 60 feet higher than its surroundings.

▲ The sun sets over the Devil's Garden.

At this point, your options are to turn around and head back to the trailhead for a total hiking mileage of 1.9 miles (2.4 miles if you took the Tunnel and Pine Tree detour) or continue north for another mile to check out Double O Arch. If you choose to do this extension, you'll head north to Double O Arch, then loop back around to the east and return hiking south along the Primitive Trail, which takes you across some challenging terrain, including one stretch along the knife-edge top of one of the sandstone fins. In all, this extension loop adds 2.9 miles of hiking, but is well worth it if you've got enough "juice"—and plenty of actual water—left for it. Indeed, Double O Arch is one of the most scenic in the park.

Whether or not you tack on Double O Arch, you won't soon forget your time walking through the Devil's Garden—and admiring Landscape Arch and all the red rock splendor of nature along the way.

CANYONLANDS NATIONAL PARK

MESA ARCH

Pinyon-juniper woodlands open up to canyon views through an iconic arch

DIFFICULTY
Easy

LOCATION
Island in the Sky, Canyonlands

LENGTH
0.7 mile

WHEELCHAIR ACCESSIBLE
No

PETS ALLOWED
No

Starvation prickly pear cacti, so nicknamed because you have to be starving to be desperate enough to try to eat them, thrive here in the red rock desert of Canyonlands, blooming out in either dusky pink or yellow flowers in late spring. ▾

No visit to Canyonlands National Park would be complete without checking out its most famous natural feature, Mesa Arch. The short loop hike to see this iconic cliff-edge arch crosses over high elevation desert terrain worthy of the old Road Runner cartoon, and is chock full of natural beauty and rich ecological interactions.

To get there, follow Grand View Point Road south from Canyonlands' Island in the Sky Visitor Center for 6 miles and turn left into the well-marked Mesa Arch Trailhead parking area. While Mesa Arch can be crowded any time of day, you'd be surprised how many people—cameras and tripods in tow—flock there at dawn when the rising sun glows off the bottom of the arch. The trail is rough and critters abound, including the occasional midget faded rattlesnake, so watch where you step.

Mesa Arch overlooks Buck Canyon with the La Sal Mountains in the distance.

Above, from left: Needle and thread, blackbrush, and Indian ricegrass are three of the most common groundcovers you'll encounter on the short hike out to Mesa Arch.

Pick up the trail right from the edge of the parking area and go right at the fork to follow it counterclockwise to get most of the hike's modest elevation gain out of the way at the beginning of the loop. Like elsewhere across canyon country, it's important to stay on the trail so as not to disrupt the fragile cryptobiotic soil layer that covers much of the sandy expanse of the Four Corners region. This black crust on the ground is composed of a vital mixture of lichens, mosses, fungi, and algae, but takes on a life of its own in preventing soil erosion and helping support larger plants.

As you hike, a profusion of desert plants will be there to keep you company. Needle and thread, blackbrush, Indian ricegrass, broom snakeweed, narrowleaf yucca, desert globemallow, woolly locoweed, green ephedra, starvation prickly pear cactus, and littleleaf mountain mahogany are a few of the more common plants down at ground and shrub levels, while pinyon pine, Utah juniper, and single-leaf ash trees rise up taller to claim first dibs on incoming sunlight.

Another major player out here is the community of lichens that dominate just about every rock surface within sight. Lichens are uniquely adapted to thrive where no other organisms can—clinging to a rock face extracting nutrients mostly from the passing breeze—and as such qualify as one of the most widespread life-forms on the planet. They are not just one organism but a form of mutual symbiosis between two different species, a fungus and an algae or cyanobacteria. The body of a lichen can be considered a small ecosystem unto itself, as it's composed of fungal filaments around cells of green algae and/or blue-green cyanobacteria. The fungus provides its partner with protection and gets nutrients in return, much in the same way that fungi and tree roots work symbiotically below the forest floor for mutual benefit. Even though they are technically a dual-species organism, lichens are classified as members of the Fungi kingdom because the fungal partner is the dominant player, while the algae or cyanobacteria is secondary.

Below, from top: At least three different types of lichen colonize this Canyonlands rock face.

Green ephedra is also known as Mormon's tea because early Mormon pioneers steeped its twigs in boiling water and drank the resulting concoction for medicinal purposes. It grows big and bushy when it finds a spot it likes.

Keep moving and at about 0.3 mile the trail will begin to slope down as you get closer to the edge of Buck Canyon. In another 0.1 mile, head right at the fork and down onto the sandstone where Mesa Arch, in all of its low-slung-but-27-foot-wide glory, comes into view. You'll want to walk around and check it out from all available angles, and thrill seekers can venture under the arch or even walk on top of it—but beware that

Above, from left: Littleleaf mountain mahogany, named after its hard mahogany-like inner red wood that Native Americans used to make tools, plays an important role in the ecosystem here. Its root nodules host bacteria that convert airborne nitrogen into a natural form of fertilizer that other plants can readily utilize.

Pinyon pines can branch out twice as wide as their height when given the opportunity to stretch out.

a slip could lead to a 500-plus foot fall down the steep cliffside into Buck Canyon.

Most of the arches across canyon country are either cliff-wall arches or freestanding arches, but Mesa Arch is what geologists call a "pothole arch," which forms when a small depression on top of a sandstone mass erodes out and merges with an alcove on the rock face below. The resulting hole is typically smooth and rounded on top, casting light down into a room-shaped opening below, just like here at Mesa Arch.

While Mesa Arch may be the big attraction here, the panoramic views aren't too shabby either. Looking out across Buck Canyon, see if you can spot other natural landmarks, including Monster Tower, Washer Woman Arch, and Airport Tower. On a clear day (which most of them are here), you see clear across to the 12,000-plus foot snow-capped La Sal Mountains 35 miles due east on the Utah-Colorado border.

When you've had enough of Mesa Arch and the gazillion dollar view, head back up the spur trail and continue the way you were going (counterclockwise) on the loop. Cross back through pinyon-juniper woodland and in 0.3 mile you'll be back at the trailhead and ready to drive onto your next Canyonlands adventure, with Mesa Arch crossed off your bucket list.

CANYONLANDS NATIONAL PARK

GRAND VIEW POINT

Quintessential canyon-edge traverse yields epic panoramic views

DIFFICULTY
Easy

LOCATION
Island in the Sky, Canyonlands

LENGTH
1.8 miles

WHEELCHAIR ACCESSIBLE
No

PETS ALLOWED
No

Hiking to Grand View Point is a great way to experience the micro- and macrobeauty of Canyonlands. The 1.8-mile out-and-back hike features views galore down into Buck Canyon and across to the snow-capped La Sal Mountains in the distance, as well as plenty of eye candy at ground level as wildflowers and desert greenery delight the senses as far as the eye can see.

To get there, follow Grand View Point Road south from Canyonlands' Island in the Sky Visitor Center for 12.2 miles until it dead-ends at the Grand View Point parking loop. The trail, which skirts the canyon edge for its entirety, is rough in spots and includes ascending a rocky hillside and some stone steps, so wear appropriate footwear and bring more water than you think you'll need.

Pick up the well-marked trail from the southern end of the parking area and continue south for 0.1 mile via a paved pathway to a small canyon overlook that most visitors here never explore beyond. Not to disparage *most* visitors, as the view from here is pretty darn great. It's 1200 feet in elevation from where you are standing on the edge to the canyon floor below. At the bottom, Monument Basin, replete with

▲ The view into Buck Canyon from the Grand View Overlook can be mesmerizing.

all kinds of towers, fins, and walls, looks like a small city of sandstone architecture. Far in the distance and down canyon, try to spot the green riparian outlines of the Colorado River as it meanders towards its confluence with the Green River nearby. Just beyond, you can see the Needles District, another section of Canyonlands National Park famous for its needlelike hoodoos. Looking at the shapes of the eroded landforms in Buck Canyon, it's easy to lose yourself in the immersive, almost abstract scenery.

Drink in the view and then proceed onto the sandy dirt trail proper and follow it west. As you hike, different views of Buck Canyon open up showcasing the wonders of geology. Indeed, the view you are looking at here today has been 300 million years in the making. It all started with the deposition of layers and layers of sediment carried by wind and water from distant mountain ranges, including the ancestral Rockies and even the Appalachians, back when today's distinct continents were joined together as one giant supercontinent we now call Pangea. Ashfalls from volcanic eruptions near and far also mixed in with the sediment, giving each successive layer its own distinctive constitution and coloration. These sedimentary layers pressed down on one another, creating a geological layer cake, with most of what had been deposited over more than 280 million years hidden below the surface. There was nothing like the eroded canyon topography we see today from the Grand View Point Trail, only vast plains gently sloping toward the horizon.

But then everything changed during the Miocene Epoch (around 20 million years ago) when movement in the earth's crust drastically reformed the landscapes of North America, long separated by then from Pangea. It was at this geological inflection point that modern landforms like the Rocky Mountains, the Great Basin, and here, the Colorado Plateau, were created. Indeed, many of the rocks we can now see exposed on the floor of modern-day Buck Canyon were deposited hundreds of millions years ago at sea level—this part of Pangea was then near the coast. But today these exact same rocks sit at around a 5000-foot elevation as a result of this ancient uplift.

Below, from top: Black sagebrush is common up here on the rim.

Desert prince's plume can thrive in spots where it can get a little sunlight to itself.

Indeed, the major tectonic reshuffling during the Miocene also created cracks in the sedimentary layers where magma (hot liquid rock) rose from deep inside the Earth. In some places, the magma cooled before reaching the surface, creating veins of harder igneous rock within the surrounding sedimentary layers. When erosion worked its way through millions of layers of sedimentary buildup, these harder deposits were exposed as the seemingly isolated mountain ranges—the La Sals, Henrys, and Abajos—visible from Canyonlands today.

Of course, the powers of erosion sculpted a lot more around here than a few isolated mountain ranges. As the uplift raised the land higher and higher over millions

of years, the Green and Colorado rivers that had initially deposited sediment millions and millions of years earlier began to take it away from the emerging plateau. Meanwhile, seasonal monsoon rains were hard at work scouring the landscape further, dissolving softer rocks and leaving exposed shelves of harder rock behind, making some of the canyon walls look like stairsteps for giants. Every now and again slabs of harder rock protected weaker layers below from eroding out, creating "balanced" rocks and towers. Another erosional factor, water seeping into cracks in the rock and then freezing and thawing repeatedly, resulted in fissures that ultimately widened out until only thin spires of rock remained.

The result that we can see here today of all this torment over millions and millions of years is modern-day Buck Canyon, filled as it is with a plethora of natural monuments, sculptures, and other proto-architectural structures. But the erosion hasn't stopped; the geological features people like you and me flock here to see today are sure to eventually disappear as new wonders take their place.

Keep moving and see how many different kinds of plants you can spot. The floral diversity here is surprising given the dry and seemingly desolate landscape. But the plants that do survive here have evolved over the eons to adapt to the environmental conditions they are born into. Green ephedra, black sagebrush, wax currant, narrowleaf yucca, Torrey's jointfir, desert prince's plume, salt heliotrope, and desert paintbrush are just a few of the low-lying plants

Top left: Wax currant occupies prime real estate at the edge of Buck Canyon.

Above: Hikers descend stone steps along the Grand View Point Trail.

you'll pass by on the hike to Grand View Point. Meanwhile, ponderosa pine trees are more common here than in other lower elevation sections of Utah, but the most common tree around these parts is the Utah juniper.

The ultimate desert survivor, Utah junipers are everywhere around the Four Corners. One of the tree's evolutionary adaptations to help it survive so many waterless months is to send down a single taproot as far as 15 feet below the sandy surface, as well as lateral roots that can extend 100 feet or more away, in order to access deep underground aquifers. Another of the tree's concessions to the desert is to "self-prune" (that is, drop) some branches when there isn't enough water to go around. Also, these junipers have especially hardy roots: even if the tree gets knocked down in a windstorm, it may well keep growing as what's below the surface isn't affected.

◂ A Utah juniper's life here at Canyonlands is full of twists and turns.

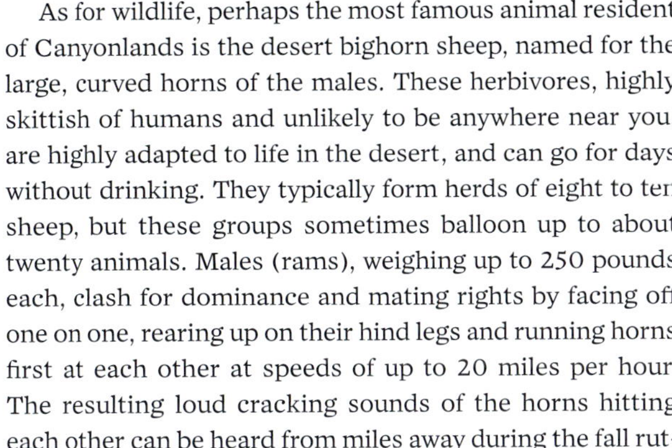

As for wildlife, perhaps the most famous animal resident of Canyonlands is the desert bighorn sheep, named for the large, curved horns of the males. These herbivores, highly skittish of humans and unlikely to be anywhere near you, are highly adapted to life in the desert, and can go for days without drinking. They typically form herds of eight to ten sheep, but these groups sometimes balloon up to about twenty animals. Males (rams), weighing up to 250 pounds each, clash for dominance and mating rights by facing off one on one, rearing up on their hind legs and running horns first at each other at speeds of up to 20 miles per hour. The resulting loud cracking sounds of the horns hitting each other can be heard from miles away during the fall rutting season. While this "sport" may seem dangerous, the animals' thick skulls cushion their brains from the impact—and the winner gets the girl.

Below, from top: Desert bighorn sheep have roamed this part of the world for 600,000 years.

Much of the "trail" underfoot consists of slowly eroding sandstone slabs.

Only about 350 individuals from this iconic Southwest species remain today within the borders of the national park, although more than 2 million of them once roamed across the region. Their demise started at the hands of white settlers during the nineteenth century who overexploited local populations as well as cut into the animals' traditional habitat. Adding insult to injury were the discovery and widespread mining of large veins of uranium buried beneath the Colorado Plateau beginning in the late 1940s. Within two decades only a small population of desert bighorns was holding on in southeast Utah.

When Canyonlands was established in 1964, only about 100 bighorns remained in the park. Realizing the magnitude of the problem, park officials phased out grazing allotments within park boundaries, as domestic sheep that had been sharing rangeland in the park were

▲ Green ephedra tucks into a little rock grotto on the edge of the canyon rim.

passing on pathogens that wild bighorns weren't evolved to handle. Meanwhile, the Bureau of Land Management limited grazing leases to cattle only on the lands it manages that border the national park, further reducing the risk of exposure to diseases brought in by domestic sheep.

These efforts helped, and by the 1980s biologists were relocating desert bighorns born and bred in Canyonlands to establish new herds in other parts of the animals' former range across Utah. This program—which involves netting Canyonlands' sheep from a helicopter and then assessing their health, age, and suitability for transport before depositing them in a new home—has reestablished viable desert bighorn populations in Arches and Capitol Reef national parks and Glen Canyon National Recreation Area. Meanwhile, bighorns relocated from here to the remote San Rafael Swell some 50 miles to the northwest have done so well as to be split into two distinct herds totaling more than 600 animals. While they are nowhere near their former population size before white settlement, desert bighorns now number some 350 animals in Canyonlands and upwards of 3000 altogether in Utah.

▲ Desert paintbrush blooms dot the landscape in red in spring and early summer.

Of course, conservationists are keeping their eyes on the prize, as increased human activity throughout the bustling Four Corners region—including not only mining and other resource exploitation but also the widespread development of housing units, office buildings, strip malls, and big box stores—poses an ongoing threat to wildlife like desert bighorns that require lots of untrammeled wilderness in order to thrive. That said, the state of Utah enacted its Bighorn Sheep Statewide Management Plan in 2013 to help maintain and grow populations statewide. This program, which brought together policymakers, ranchers, biologists, conservationists, and government officials to work together on bighorn sheep conservation, was deemed a success during a five-year trial run and subsequently renewed in 2018 for another ten years. Time will tell if desert bighorns can rebound even more than they already have, especially in the face of still-increasing human encroachment on their wild domain.

As for other wildlife here at Canyonlands, mountain lions and mule deer are constantly playing their own version of cat-and-mouse around the ledges and slopes, with the rise and fall of each animal's annual population numbers here directly linked to one another. (In Utah, mule deer makes up 80 percent of the mountain lion's diet.) Black bears pass through in late summer and fall foraging for berries and other goodies primarily in the riparian zones along the Colorado and Green rivers.

Rodents here include white-tailed antelope ground squirrels, pinyon mice, desert woodrats, Hopi chipmunks, and rock squirrels, while desert cottontails and black-tailed jackrabbits represent the lagomorphs. And like anywhere with lots of canyon walls and rock caves, bats prevail at Canyonlands. You probably won't see them, but pallid bats, big brown bats, Allen's big-eared bats, California myotises, and fringed myotises are all common here.

Reptile lovers rejoice: you'll have a lot to love here if you are patient and know where to look. Common snakes include desert striped whipsnakes, gopher snakes, and

terrestrial garter snakes, while lizards include western whiptails, common sagebrush lizards, plateau lizards, tree lizards, and common side-blotched lizards.

Although Canyonlands isn't known as an avian hotspot, birds may be the most visible wildlife here along the Grand View Point Trail. White-throated swifts roost in the canyon wall below you and circle above in search of airborne prey. Their rapid, acrobatic flight is amazing to watch as they can turn back and forth quickly on the wing in order to harvest more insects and spiders. Meanwhile, red-tailed hawks, Cooper's hawks, American kestrels, and peregrine falcons are among the raptors commonly seen hunting over Buck Canyon. And turkey vultures may circle high above it all, scanning for unfinished leftovers from any recent mountain lion kills below.

Up here on the rim, keep an eye (and ear) out for Say's phoebes, canyon wrens, juniper titmice, black-throated sparrows, black-throated gray warblers, black-chinned hummingbirds, northern flickers, mountain chickadees, pinyon jays, scrub jays, and, of course, common ravens. The latter three species are corvids, and as such are some of the smartest birds in creation. They utilize a range of vocalizations to communicate with one another and, like only a few other animal species, are able to plan ahead and process complex tasks.

Above left: Canyonlands National Park, with all of its caves and overhangs, is a veritable haven for bats.

▲ Junction Butte from the Grand View Point Trail

Keep moving and soon enough you'll reach the end of the trail at a small overlook on the very southern tip of the plateau. Take in the panorama, which includes Buck Canyon, Junction Butte, and the confluence of the Green and Colorado rivers 8 miles to the south. When you've had enough of this endless view, turn around and retrace your steps for the 0.9 mile back to the trailhead, confident that you now know just what makes Canyonlands tick.

CANYONLANDS NATIONAL PARK

UPHEAVAL DOME

Steep hike through pinyon-juniper woodland to a mysterious dome

	DIFFICULTY Moderate
LOCATION Island in the Sky, Canyonlands	LENGTH 1.3 miles
WHEELCHAIR ACCESSIBLE No	PETS ALLOWED No

The short hike to Upheaval Dome showcases a geological phenomenon that still has experts baffled to this day as to its cause. A short but sometimes steep hike leads to two different overlooks of this anomalous but nevertheless scenic rock formation.

Opposite: How Upheaval Dome formed is still a mystery to geologists.

Below, from top: Sego lilies are not only beautiful but edible; their bulbs helped sustain Mormon pioneers during food shortages.

The yellow blooms of Ives' four-nerved daisy seem to alight from a crevice in the rock.

To get there, follow Grand View Point Road south from Canyonlands' Island in the Sky Visitor Center for 6.3 miles and then turn right (west) and follow Upheaval Dome Road for 4.8 miles until it dead-ends at a circular parking loop by the Upheaval Dome Trailhead. The trail ascends on a sometimes sandy, slippery trail marked only by the occasional rock cairn and the footsteps of others up to two different overlooks, so wear sturdy footwear and be prepared to climb.

Start out at the trailhead at the west end of the parking area and follow the spur trail for 300 feet. Then go right at the fork onto the well-marked Upheaval Dome Trail. Pass through quintessential pinyon-juniper woodland along the way. If it's spring, a host of colorful wildflower blooms will keep you company. Sego lilies, in all their dusky pink and yellow glory, are particularly beautiful but also are a delicacy for rodents, bears, and desert bighorn sheep, not to mention Native Americans who would dig up the plant's bulbs and eat them either raw or roasted. Indeed, Mormon pioneers learned from their Indigenous neighbors that sego lily bulbs could provide quite a tasty and nutritious treat during times when other food was hard to come by. Other cheerful blooms of springtime come from Navajo fleabane, desert globemallow,

and Ives' four-nerved daisy, while big bushes of Apache plume spread out in the sandy gaps.

After approximately 0.3 mile, take the short turnoff trail to the right (north) to the first overlook. This vantage point offers a stunning panoramic view of Upheaval Dome and its surrounding cliffs and canyon. No one can be sure what caused this strange geological arrangement before you, but one theory holds that a meteorite or asteroid with a diameter of about 0.3 mile struck Earth at what is now Upheaval Dome. According to this theory, the impact would have caused a huge explosion, sending dust and debris high into the atmosphere and causing the rocks at the site to fracture and deform, resulting in the distinctive circular structure we see today at Upheaval Dome. The central uplift and surrounding rim are believed to be the result of the rebound of rocks following the impact. Evidence supporting the "impact crater" theory includes the presence of shocked quartz and other impact-related minerals found in the rocks surrounding Upheaval Dome, as well as the circular shape and central uplift characteristic of impact craters.

The other leading theory contends that Upheaval Dome is the result of a salt dome formation. Salt deposits deep beneath the Earth's surface are known to flow over time due to their low viscosity under pressure. As these salt deposits moved, they caused the overlying rock layers to buckle and deform, creating a dome-shaped structure. Over millions of years, the overlaying rock layers eroded away, exposing the underlying salt dome. According to this theory, Upheaval Dome's central uplift and surrounding rim are believed to be remnants of this original prehistoric salt dome structure. Whether or not geologists will ever attain consensus on how Upheaval Dome formed is anybody's guess, but regardless it sure is weird to see it here in the middle of this otherworldly national park.

Once you've taken some time to soak in the breathtaking scenery and wrap your head around the unique geology in front of you, head onward to the second overlook by getting back to the main trail and continuing west. At first, the trail dips into a little gully, and then it rises again on the way to the second viewpoint. This section of the trail is slightly more rugged, with some rocky sections, uneven terrain, and lots of loose scree. Keep an eye out for rock cairns to

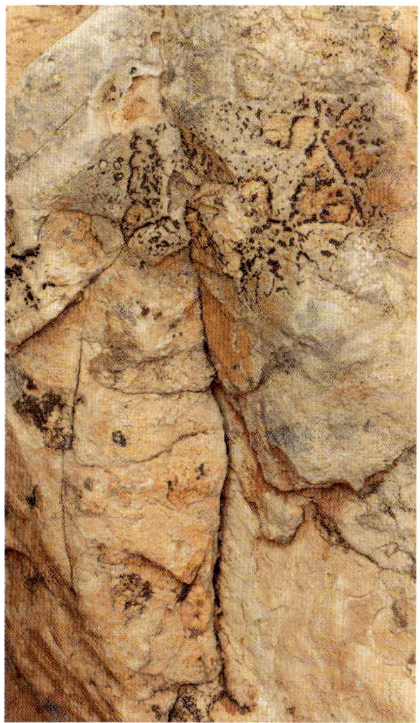

Clockwise, from above: This tormented sandstone rock face has seen millions of years of history pass it by.

Navajo fleabane is a daisy relative that thrives in the dry and sandy soil of the desert.

Desert globemallow lights up the shrub layer with its showy orange blooms.

help guide you along the path and be sure to watch your step as you make your way up. The extra hiking distance is well worth the trouble as you'll gain a different perspective on the Upheaval Dome and add some extra "steps" to your pedometer in the process.

When you've appreciated this true geological wonder to the extent of your abilities, turn around and carefully make your way mostly downhill back to the trailhead, a little more enlightened, yet filled with wonder about our beautiful, dynamic, and still so wild and mysterious world.

CAPITOL REEF NATIONAL PARK

GRAND WASH

Narrow rock canyon gorge with 800-foot walls and diverse flora

DIFFICULTY
Easy

LOCATION
Central Capitol Reef

LENGTH
2.5 miles

WHEELCHAIR ACCESSIBLE
No

PETS ALLOWED
No

A short hike into Capitol Reef's Grand Wash gets you up close and personal with more than 200 million years of geology while you traverse a beautiful canyon gorge replete with natural rock wall sculptures and oasis-like desert greenery.

◂ The vertical lines on these sandstone walls come from a microbial coating called rock varnish that tends to form on rock faces in arid environments.

▾ A hiker makes his way past Mother Nature's rock art on the way through the Grand Wash.

While you can walk the entire length of the Grand Wash from the southern trailhead off Capitol Reef's Scenic Road to the northern terminus 2.3 miles to the north at Utah State Route 24 (UT-24), you'd have to walk back the way you came, making for a 4.6-mile out-and-back hike—or arrange for a car shuttle to drop you back at your starting point. If you don't have access to a second car for a shuttle and/or you don't have the juice for almost 5 miles of hiking, you can hike into the Grand Wash from the south for a little over a mile to see the spectacular middle Narrows section and then turn around and head back the way you came for a total hiking distance of less than 2.5 miles. And

a warning to the wise: if there are any signs of rain, thunder, or lightning, save the Grand Wash for another day. Canyons like this fill up with torrential waves of water and wood and rock during heavy rain events, and you wouldn't want to be caught inside. But most days in the desert are sunny and clear and you'll have nothing to fear.

To get there from the Capitol Reef National Park Visitor Center off of UT-24, follow Scenic Drive as it meanders south and east for 3.4 miles and then turn left (north) and follow Grand Wash Road to its terminus at a small parking area with pit toilets in 1.3 miles. The obvious trail starts pronto, heading further north and east into the depths of the canyon.

As you hike in, you can't help but stare up in awe at the grandeur of the canyon walls surrounding you. The cliffs along the Grand Wash stand some 700-plus feet tall—about the height of a 50-story building. The Grand Wash started its life as a fissure in a 200 million-year-old rock wall. Over time, monsoon rains repeatedly filled the gully with torrents of water and debris, routing it into the deep canyon we know and love today. It's still risky to be caught in the middle of the Grand Wash, or any other so-called "slot canyons," during a heavy rainstorm; indeed, the erosion process is ongoing here.

When it's not raining, though, a "wash," by definition, remains dry—and is safe to hike through. Keep moving north and stop to admire all of the eroded sandstone walls, full of pockmarks, alcoves, potholes, windows, and striations. These rocks look like they have been through a lot, but in reality a lot has been through them.

▾ Rose heath is one of the many kinds of wildflowers making a living here at the bottom of the Grand Wash.

When you're not staring at the abstractions of the walls of the canyon, check out some of the flora vying for soil and sunlight here at what seems like the bottom of the world. Big healthy bushes of Apache plume thrive in the dynamic environment of the wash, while cliffrose gives off a sweet scent that attracts bees and other pollinators—and is an important browse plant for the occasional mule deer and desert bighorn sheep that wander into the wash. Rubber rabbitbrush is also a key player down here

Above, from top:
A hiker enjoys a peaceful moment under a rock wall alongside the Grand Wash Trail.

A mushroom rock in the making with a more erosion-resistant tip than body.

at ground level. Meanwhile, Utah penstemon, woolly locoweed, rough mule's ears, Navajo fleabane, desert willow, and tufted evening primrose are among the other shrub layer plants making cameos here and there throughout the wash.

At about a mile into the hike the side walls begin to close in and soon enough you enter the Narrows, where the canyon is only 20 feet wide. The high-pitched rattling scree sound of white-throated swifts preying on flying insects in the air column above you is a little disarming. Hopefully you can't even imagine the force of running water through this narrowest section of the canyon during a monsoon rain event. Even in the middle of a bright sunny day, it sure is dark in this narrowest half-mile stretch of the wash, with the canyon walls closing in so tight as to block out most of the sun's rays. Linger here as long as you like and then turn around and go back the way you came (unless you are doing a thru-hike or car shuttle, in which case, continue north to the trailhead along UT-24).

One thing is certain: hiking the Grand Wash is one way to cement your understanding of how canyon geology works, and to immerse yourself in one of Mother Nature's true temples.

CAPITOL REEF NATIONAL PARK

GOOSENECKS OVERLOOK AND SUNSET POINT

Overlooks of eroded cliffs showcase what a little creek can do if given 60 million years

DIFFICULTY
Easy

LOCATION
Central Capitol Reef

LENGTH
0.8 mile

WHEELCHAIR ACCESSIBLE
No

PETS ALLOWED
No

Stopping for a quick jaunt out to Goosenecks Overlook and Sunset Point for a view down into the canyon carved by Sulphur Creek is a must-do for any visitor to Capitol Reef National Park.

To get there from the Capitol Reef National Park Visitor Center, drive west on Utah State Route 24 (UT-24) for 2.4 miles and then turn left (south) onto Panorama Point Road and continue straight past the Panorama Point parking area onto Goosenecks Road, a graded dirt road that's rough in spots but passable, for another 0.8 mile until it dead-ends at the well-marked Goosenecks Point parking area.

Park and follow the well-marked trail at the south end of the parking area to Goosenecks Overlook. The short path winds through the rocky cliffside expanse for 0.1 mile until it opens up to the overlook itself, with views down into the canyon of the twisted and contorted "gooseneck"-shaped cliffs carved over the ages by small Sulphur Creek. An unassuming double-runged metal railing is all that's keeping you or your little ones from falling to a near certain death 800 feet down into the chasm below, so watch your step.

◂ Looking down at one of the "gooseneck" turns in Sulphur Creek some 800 feet below makes you appreciate the power of water as an agent of change.

It certainly is hard to believe that a stream as diminutive and unassuming as Sulphur Creek, today far below at the bottom of the canyon, could wear away hundreds of millions of years—and 800-plus feet in elevation—worth of sedimentary rock deposits. But you can't argue with physics, and the layered geological proof is right here before your eyes. (Lucky you.)

How the gooseneck curves of the canyon formed is still a matter of debate among geologists. Were they superimposed or subsequent to the formation of the canyon? One theory holds that a meandering prehistoric Sulphur Creek developed on a relatively flat-lying land surface thousands of feet above the spot we are now standing on. According to this theory, the creek cut downward over tens of millions of years, superimposing its

▾ The common sagebrush lizard is one of the most common of the nine lizard species present in Capitol Reef National Park.

meandering pattern on the rock layers below, all the way down to the bottom of the canyon as we know it today.

The other predominant theory is that the goosenecks formed subsequent to the creek cutting into the rock layers. As this theory goes, the creek would have intersected with preexisting angular fractures in the sandstone along the way. The stream would have then followed the new course of the fractures, creating a new flow route subsequent to the original one.

Regardless of how these goosenecks formed, you can't help but admire the power of erosion and the grandeur of nature in looking out over this spectacular scene. When you've had enough of the mesmerizing view, turn around and head back to the parking area where you can pick up the other trail there leading east for 0.3 mile through stunning red rock desert scenery to Sunset Point. Utah junipers, pinyon pines, and the occasional ponderosa pine are the only

▲ Roundleaf buffaloberry, seen here clinging to a cliff edge near the Goosenecks Overlook, "fixes" nitrogen—that is, it hosts bacteria on its roots that convert airborne nitrogen into an all-natural chemical fertilizer that other plants can use to help them grow.

flora taller than a few feet high out here on this exposed mesa top. Meanwhile, a coterie of other drought-tolerant native plants—black sagebrush, Torrey's jointfir, roundleaf buffaloberry, and green ephedra, among others—fill in the occasional gap or crack in the otherwise endless overlapping slabs of sandstone.

While this rather desolate spot of desert isn't the biggest draw for wildlife, you may well hear some birdsong from the likes of rock wrens, spotted towhees, or pinyon jays. White-throated swifts nest in cavities in the cliffs below and forage on the wing for insect treats, sometimes treating nearby cliff-top hikers to a dazzling air show. Meanwhile, peregrine falcons and golden eagles ride the air shafts as they scope for prey far below on the canyon floor.

Soon before you reach the terminus at Sunset Point the trail jogs out onto the edge of the canyon, where one wrong step could be a tragedy—so be careful. The trail then cuts up and back "inland" slightly to the local high spot, Sunset Point itself, on top of some sandstone boulders. From this perch you can see for hundreds of miles on a clear day in every direction.

To the west, Fremont Gorge backs up to piney Bluebell Knoll. Snow-capped Mount Dutton, elevation 11,041 feet, looms on the horizon some 50 miles beyond. Looking north, Chimney Rock stands solitary as sandstone walls recede into the distance behind it, following the northward course of the Waterpocket Fold, the 100-mile-long geological rift that encompasses Capitol Reef National Park.

The view to the east tracks a series of "gooseneck" cliffs—created way back when Sulphur Creek was just getting started carving the canyon now 800 feet below—as they rise uphill, terminating at a panorama of Capitol Reef's famous Fluted Wall. This massive red sandstone bulkhead is in the middle of a process of erosion started some 240 million years ago when the brick-red Moenkopi sandstone sediments making up the bottom stripe of the wall's "layer cake" were deposited. Following on the heels of the Moenkopi deposit some 15 million years later was the deposition of the gray-green and purple Chinle Formation, and then 25 million years later the (now mostly eroded) Wingate Sandstone deposit on top. The reason this wall looks "fluted" is that over time water and ice flowing rapidly over

The Fluted Wall as seen from Sunset Point a mile away

▲ A pinyon pine and a few black sagebrush bushes crop up in the sandy soil between sandstone slabs.

the steep edges of the cliffs carried away soft and loose particles of sandstone, leaving the underlying harder, thicker, erosion-resistant sandstone to show through. These days the Fluted Wall towers some 700 vertical feet above the valley below it.

A little further south, look for another eroded sandstone formation called the Navajo Knobs, and beyond that, 30 miles to the southeast of Sunset Point, the Henry Mountains, capped off by 11,413-foot Mount Pennell. No matter where you look, you'll be hard-pressed to find a bad view.

If you've timed your visit for sunset, get ready for the sinking orb to light up the surrounding cliff walls in glowing red light—and make sure your camera is ready. And if you linger late you'll be treated to some of the darkest skies in the Lower 48 and whatever stars and constellations you can make out up there. In fact, in 2015, Capitol Reef was recognized by DarkSky International with its "Dark Sky Park" designation—so turn off your flashlight and just look up. But whatever time of day you visit, the views from Goosenecks Overlook and Sunset Point won't disappoint.

When it's time to go, retrace your steps the 0.3 mile back to the Goosenecks Overlook parking area and drive the short dirt road back toward civilization, that much more in awe of the power and beauty of Mother Nature.

CAPITOL REEF NATIONAL PARK

SULPHUR CREEK WATERFALL

Lush riparian ecosystem and unique waterslide waterfall, but also quintessential Capitol Reef

DIFFICULTY
Easy to moderate

LOCATION
Central Capitol Reef

LENGTH
1.4 miles

WHEELCHAIR ACCESSIBLE
No

PETS ALLOWED
No

This 1.4-mile out-and-back hike along the muddy banks of scenic Sulphur Creek crosses through a lush riparian ecosystem on its way to a small and pleasant waterfall that those young at heart will delight in sliding down on a hot summer day. Plus, if you've seen Sulphur Creek from on high—like from the Goosenecks Overlook—you'll appreciate being down along, and even in, this small but mighty tributary of the Colorado River that has carved out much of the finest scenery as far as the eye can see.

To get there, park in the gravel parking area on the north side of Utah State Route 24 (UT-24) just west of the Capitol Reef National Park Visitor Center. Cross over the road and pick up the well-marked Sulphur Creek Trail at the north end of the parking lot and follow it as it leads around and behind the visitor center building and crosses Sulphur Creek. The water rarely gets higher than midcalf along this stretch of the creek (except after a heavy rain, when you should steer clear anyway). You may want to bring sandals and a small towel along for this and a few other creek crossings you'll have to negotiate along the way, or just wear shoes or sneakers you don't mind getting wet.

While you may not see them in the reddish-brown water, bluehead suckers and southern leatherside chubs are among the fish living in Sulphur Creek. The former, considered by the state of Utah to be a sensitive species, is native to this Colorado River system and likes to scrape algae, its main form of sustenance, off rocks on the creek bottom. Meanwhile, the southern leatherside chub is not native to the river system and causes problems by outcompeting native fish.

Once you've crossed the river, head straight across the desert plain in front of you, with Capitol Reef's famous formation called the Castle on display to the north. After about 300 feet the sandy and often faint trail—following others' footprints is your best bet to stay on track—leads you along the north bank of Sulphur Creek.

As you hike, keep an eye out for smooth, round black igneous rocks scattered to and fro around the landscape. Geologists have traced them back to 20 million-year-old lava flows out of the Boulder and Thousand Lakes mountains 15 miles west of here. At the end of the last ice age, 10,000 to 15,000 years ago, melting, moving glaciers eroded much of that hard lava rock, with glacier meltwater and debris flows transporting chunks, large and small, downhill and many miles from their place of birth, so to speak. The black rocks you see here today probably were plugging up one of those formerly active volcanoes for millions of years before taking a rough-and-tumble journey here, hitching a ride in gritty floodwaters that sanded them so smooth.

After about 0.3 mile of hiking, look for a historic lime kiln slightly uphill to the north. Settlers in the pioneer community of Fruita just a mile down the road built the kiln around 1900 to make lime, which they used as a substrate for producing mortar and cement and as an acidity-lowering soil additive to boost their agricultural yields. They would also whitewash the trunks of young fruit trees in the community's orchard with lime to deter pillaging rodents and insects. The National Park Service rehabilitated the kiln in 2015, using historic photographs to guide the replacement of individual stones after decades of neglect had taken a toll. The kiln is now part of the Fruita Rural Historic District

Opposite, clockwise from top: Fremont cottonwood trees dot the banks of Sulphur Creek.

A wasp alights on golden crownbeard's yellow bloom.

Igneous rocks are backed up by the Castle, one of the iconic rock formations of Capitol Reef National Park.

and serves as a reminder to visitors of the self-sufficiency needed by early settlers to make a living out here in the remote and hardscrabble desert. While the kiln might look sturdy, climbing on it could damage it or cause it to collapse, so keep your distance.

Moving right along, the trail follows the winding course of the creek, including a few more crossings. Along the way, you'll see plenty of greenery hugging the banks

▲ Pioneers built this lime kiln to heat up limestone to turn it into lime to use as mortar or cement and as a soil additive.

competing for access to water, perhaps the most precious commodity out here for plants and just about any other living thing. Given that Capitol Reef doesn't get more than 8 inches of rain in a typical year, Sulphur Creek, which flows year-round, is kind of an oasis in the desert.

Along this hike you get a front and center view of the profusion of plant life here. Rubber rabbitbrush is omnipresent; black-tailed jackrabbits use it for cover and as forage. Indian ricegrass and tarragon freely intermingle at ankle height along the trailside. Apache plume, scarlet globemallow, fragrant sumac, sneezeweed hymenoxys, desert prince's plume, golden crownbead, four-wing saltbush, plateau penstemon, pale evening primrose, roundleaf buffaloberry, and three kinds of cacti (starvation prickly pear, small-flower fishhook, and claret cup) are among the plant species you may get to see along the trail.

And hanging over it all are the graceful boughs of Fremont cottonwood trees. These water-loving trees native to the desert Southwest provide perches and nesting habitat for all kinds of birds—warbling vireos, Bullock's orioles,

Above, from left: Apache plume produces unique flowers in late spring.

Plateau penstemon lends some purple flair to the otherwise red rock and green landscape.

hairy woodpeckers, northern flickers—as well as cover and shade for a host of mammals including mule deer, rock squirrels, ringtails, and an assortment of rodents.

And where there are cottonwoods, there's usually beaver. Indeed, North America's largest rodent uses the tree's branches and limbs not only as food but also as lumber for its industrious construction projects—and here along Sulphur Creek is no exception. Unlike elsewhere, where beavers construct elaborate dams or lodges right in the waterway, here they build dens in the stream bank. Biologists still aren't sure why, but one theory holds that occasional high flow rates during monsoon season flash floods can undo all of a beaver community's hard work in building up their dams and lodges, so instead the smarties here live in safer digs just out of harm's way. While you're unlikely to see beavers on your visit to Capitol Reef, you could find evidence of their presence here along the stream banks in the form of tracks and chewed or downed trees.

Keep moving and soon enough, after about 0.7 mile of hiking, the creek and trail curve around to the right and there in front of you is little Sulphur Creek Falls, which drops about 6 feet off a sandstone ledge into a small, shallow pool. If it's a warm summer day, you'll definitely have company here, typically in the form of family groups with lots of ecstatic swimming, screaming kids. While you might not find the solitude you were hoping for here, you may as well join the fun. Anyone can slide down the waterfall and dunk in the pool below; why not you?

◂ Sulphur Creek Falls

When you've experienced the small falls to your heart's content, turn around and retrace your steps along the creek back to the trailhead. You can cut across the desert plain like you did on the way out or follow the course of the river during that stretch for a slightly different set of views. Whichever return route you choose, you'll be glad you made the time to check out this most unique but also quintessential Capitol Reef National Park hike.

BRYCE CANYON NATIONAL PARK

SUNRISE POINT TO SUNSET POINT

Paved walk along the western rim of Bryce Canyon yields otherworldly hoodoo views

DIFFICULTY
Easy

LOCATION
Central Bryce Canyon

LENGTH
1 mile

WHEELCHAIR ACCESSIBLE
Yes

PETS ALLOWED
Yes

A more scenic walk one cannot imagine. This mile-long jaunt along the western rim of Bryce Canyon's natural amphitheater yields not only grand views across the red rock hoodoo expanse but also a primer in the desert ecology of south-central Utah.

You can start out on either end of this heavenly half-mile stretch of paved pathway between Sunrise and Sunset points, forming the central and most visited section of Bryce's Rim Trail, which that extends for 5.5 miles in total between Bryce Point to the south and Fairyland Point up north. You won't be alone on the walk, given the stunning view of Bryce Amphitheater and the central location, just a few steps away from the park's lodging and dining facilities and parking lots. Indeed, this section of the Rim Trail is perhaps the most visited spot in all of Bryce Canyon National Park. But despite the crowds, you'll feel like it's just you and the hoodoo-filled canyon as you stare out over the edge. (That said, your best bet for less people around is sunrise.)

Sunrise is an ideal time to be on the Rim Trail at Bryce Canyon if you want to see the "pink cliffs" at their most colorful.

Starting from the north at Sunrise Point, hike up to the viewpoint that rises above the expansive 36-square-mile, 800-foot-deep Bryce Amphitheater to your east. Thousands and thousands of minaret-like red rock hoodoos—formed by eroding sandstone—dominate the view to the east.

Bryce's unique topography began to develop some 144 million years ago during what geologists call the Cretaceous Period. Over a period of 60 million years, a 10,000-square-mile lake (bigger than present day Lake Erie) extended from the southeast into the area we know today as Bryce Canyon, depositing sediments of varying thickness with each repeated inundation and subsequent retreat. These successive waves of sediment deposition built up thousands of feet thick, with the remnants still visible to this day as the gray-brown rocks at the very bottom of the canyon.

Bryce's signature pink cliffs, which sit on top of the older, aforementioned gray-brown Cretaceous base layer, began to form 40 to 60 million years ago in the Tertiary Period, when highlands to the west eroded into shallow, broad basins as deposits of limey, iron-rich sediments—known as the Claron Formation—filled in under a series of lakes and streams. These so-called Claron deposits, tinted salmon pink in hue due to the high iron content, are what eventually eroded into the pink cliffs (and hoodoos) that have made Bryce famous.

This erosion process certainly didn't happen overnight. As the sediments hardened over eons into the rock we see today (via a geological process called lithification), joints formed, similar to how cracks appear in mud as it dries. A prehistoric period of seismic activity further widened and deepened these joints. (The region is seismically dormant these days.) From there, the erosive power of water did the rest to create the Bryce Amphitheater that nowadays draws 1.5 million human visitors to the rim every year.

Spindly Rocky Mountain junipers adorn the rim edge. ▾

At Bryce, winter snows melt a little bit during the heat of the day, dripping into the joints in the sandstone, where it then freezes at night and expands, breaking the adjacent rock into smaller

▲ A dramatic ponderosa pine tree spreads its branches out over the rim of Bryce Canyon.

pieces in a process known as frost wedging. Bryce gets some 170 days a year of freeze-thaw conditions; as such, frost wedging is still a major erosive factor in the amphitheater's ongoing formation.

Running water has been another major player in the creation of Bryce Canyon's current good looks. Indeed, ancient rivers and streams sliced deep gullies into the eastern wall of the plateau, carving out what we now refer to as "rock fins"—sometimes with slot canyons on either or both sides, depending on surrounding near-field geologic conditions. In some cases, windows or arches can form in these fins as they erode away.

Contemplate the otherworldly view from this advantageous vantage point to your heart's content, and then proceed south along the Rim Trail. It may be hard to take your eyes off the gazillion dollar view out over the canyon, but the details down at your feet are just as amazing, albeit humbler.

Bryce sits at the top of the Paunsagunt Plateau, which rises out of southwest Utah's high desert. This elevated spot gets significantly more rain than the surrounding desert lowlands below and also stays cooler in summer. As a result, Bryce sports greater floral diversity than the surrounding desert and feels accordingly lush by comparison.

The most common tree you'll see all over the rim as well as in choice spots down into the canyon is the ponderosa pine. This Great Basin stalwart—common across the Intermountain West from southern Canada on into northern Mexico—is recognizable by its orange-tinted bark broken up into crude jigsaw puzzle patterns. The tree produces slender 10-inch needles that grow in bundles of three and large egg-shaped reddish-brown cones. Stick your nose into the gaps in the bark and enjoy the sweet smell emanating from the tree's sap. Some liken it to butterscotch while others say vanilla, but whatever it smells like, what's not to like?

Another tree that thrives along the rim is Rocky Mountain juniper. It's not to be confused with its shorter, stouter cousin Utah juniper, which prefers slightly lower elevations and as such can be found in greater numbers down within Bryce Canyon. Rocky Mountain juniper is right at home in the more refined air at the rim's elevation of 7900 feet. They can grow as tall as 50 feet, but a third or half that height is more typical here along Bryce's exposed rim. This slender-branched, gnarly barked, reddish-brown tree sports short gray-green needles and bright blue berrylike cones with a frosty white coating. While humans may complain that the tree's little "berries" taste bitter, a wide range of birds and rodents certainly seem to like them. The seeds are indigestible and eliminated as waste when eaten by these animals. But the process of passing through their guts softens the seeds' coats, jolting them out of dormancy and kickstarting the germination process.

Look lower to the ground on the rim between the big pines and junipers and you'll find greenleaf manzanita. These hardy shrubs grow only 2 to 3 feet tall up here but spread out some three times as wide, filling in many a sandy gap. You'll know this shrub from its unlobed, smooth-edged leathery green leaves, each about the size of a quarter, and its rough-hewn reddish-brown bark. In spring, these manzanitas produce small clusters of light pink urn-shaped flowers with a striking resemblance to heather, one of the manzanita's closest high-country relatives (both are members of the heath family). In late summer and early fall, the plant's flowers give way to green berries that quickly ripen into a rusty-red color, signaling their ripeness to the area's deer, rodents, and birds.

Above, from top:
Greenleaf manzanita is a major understory player in the forest that skirts Bryce's rim.

Don't feed the golden-mantled ground squirrels that frequently orbit hikers along Bryce's rim in search of handouts.

Another common shrub layer plant here is big sagebrush, perhaps the most ubiquitous of all the plants across the six-state region known as the Great Basin. These scrubby shrubs grow about 2 feet tall and sport small velvety blue-gray-silver leaves that give off a bittersweet aroma, which deters animals from browsing on it. The plant's leaves contain oils that herbivores cannot digest, which helps explain why it has been so successful in colonizing so much of the well-grazed high desert rangeland that covers swaths of California, Oregon, Nevada, Utah, Idaho, and Wyoming. Meanwhile, green rabbitbrush, rubber rabbitbrush, bitterbrush, and spineless horsebrush all thrive in dry, sandy conditions and make up most of the rest of the understory layer here on Bryce's rim.

If you are looking for wildlife, you may or may not get lucky enough to glimpse a mule deer or Rocky Mountain elk prancing through the forest near the rim. But chances are good a golden-mantled ground squirrel—10 inches long with stripes like a chipmunk, but not on its head—may get friendly looking for handouts. They hibernate in the winter months but also store food in their burrows for some nibbles when they wake up in spring. While they don't seem too scared of humans, these cute little squirrels should remain wary of carnivorous predators like hawks, jays, foxes, bobcats, and coyotes.

Other rodents common around Bryce's rim include Uinta chipmunks, Uinta ground squirrels, cliff chipmunks, least chipmunks, and rock squirrels. Well adapted to their surroundings, this coterie of rodents lives large off relatively scant desert plateau offerings like grasses, seeds, fungi, juniper berries, and the leaves of forbs, along with the occasional earthworm and increasingly on discarded human food and improperly secured garbage.

Birds are also common around Bryce's rim—upwards of 200 different avian species either call Bryce home or pass through during the year. Ravens are all over the place in this most crowded part of the national park, making themselves at home with human scraps. Steller's jays, Clark's nutcrackers, violet-green swallows, cedar waxwings, dark-eyed juncos, American robins, black-capped chickadees, and western tanagers are among the other birds you may encounter upon visiting Bryce if you stay alert.

Keep heading south along the rim and soon enough you'll find yourself at Sunset Point, where there is another viewing area jutting out into the canyon looking west over a sea of red rock hoodoos. If you parked back near Sunrise, retrace your steps for new perspectives onto Bryce's amphitheater. Otherwise head into Bryce Canyon Lodge, just a few steps back from the rim, where you can take the edge off with a prickly pear margarita or a bowl of elk chili. The building, designed by Gilbert Stanley Underwood and completed in 1925, features rough stonework, a wave-patterned shingle roof, and large supporting logs that match the size of the ponderosa pines surrounding it. It is truly a marvel of rustic architecture, seamlessly blending nature and nurture. There's no better place to gather your wits after a hike along the rim of Bryce Canyon.

BRYCE CANYON NATIONAL PARK

QUEEN'S GARDEN AND NAVAJO LOOP

Descend into Bryce Canyon to see iconic eroded rock formations and canyon bottom ecology

DIFFICULTY
Moderate

LOCATION
Central Bryce Canyon

LENGTH
3 miles

WHEELCHAIR ACCESSIBLE
No

PETS ALLOWED
No

If you want to get more intimate with the hoodoos of Bryce Canyon, the trail down to Queen's Garden might be just the ticket. While the 3-mile loop hike detailed here from Sunrise Point to Sunset Point via Bryce Canyon's depths and the Navajo Loop are easy for the first two-thirds, be prepared: the final climb back out of the canyon entails switchback after switchback as it rises 500-plus feet in elevation—and as such isn't for the faint-hearted.

The National Park Service recommends hiking the trail clockwise, starting at Sunrise Point and descending from there, which puts the best views of the amphitheater in front of you as you hike down (as opposed to over your shoulder as you hike out). Also, keeping most of the hiker flow one-way reduces the feeling of crowdedness on the trail, which can be a problem on this most popular of all hikes at Bryce.

The relatively wide, sandy trail leads down a series of gradual switchbacks, allowing plenty of great views out

across the hoodoo expanse and beyond. As you start to descend, you'll immediately find yourself immersed in a world of towering hoodoos and red rock bridges and tunnels sculpted by erosion over millions of years. The trail is well-maintained and gradually winds its way down into the amphitheater-like landscape, providing both stunning views and a sense of immersion in the geologic wonders around you.

▲ It sure is fun to be down among the hoodoos looking up at the tiny people on Bryce Canyon's rim.

After about 0.8 mile, you'll reach the Queen's Garden junction, where the Queen's Garden Trail intersects with the Navajo Loop Trail. Take the short side trail here by the sign pointing out the Queen Victoria hoodoo, a single hoodoo

Above, right: Queen Victoria is expected to hold court for many more years here at the bottom of Bryce Canyon.

with a formation that resembles the profile of England's queen during the late 1800s. Like the thousands of other hoodoos all around her, Queen Victoria formed as a result of a series of erosional processes over the last 50 million years or so. Back then, an iron-rich deposit of sediment known as the Claron Formation settled into what we now call Bryce Canyon. Over the ensuing eons, frost wedging—when water seeps into cracks, freezes, and expands, making the cracks ever wider as the process continues—has been a key player in the sculpting process, but acidic rainwater and myriad other weather and climate factors have also played a role. The result is the seemingly ordered beauty of Bryce's

Amphitheater, and the Queen Victoria hoodoo is a symbol for Bryce that's known all around the world. See it while you can, as it is sure to tumble down at some point in the next 50 million years.

Down here at the bottom of Bryce Canyon, plant life is relatively sparse given the seasonal temperature extremes, overall arid conditions, and erosional factors that constantly change and upset the landscape. That said, certain species find a way to eke out a living despite such challenges.

To wit, Utah junipers can "self-prune" in times of drought, cutting off the nutrient supply to one branch in order to ensure the overall tree's survival. These primarily monoecious (both sexes on the same plant) trees grow into twisted and gnarled trunks between 9 and 19 feet tall. Their pea-sized light blue berries are actually tiny cones covered in a drought-resistant waxy coating to retain moisture. Black-tailed jackrabbits, coyotes, gray foxes, cliff chipmunks, Uinta chipmunks, and lots of birds indulge in these nutrient-packed "berries," while mule deer depend on the conifer's year-round browsable foliage for sustenance during winter when the pickings are otherwise slim.

Another example of the kind of tree that thrives down here where others can't is the pinyon pine, which withstands drought by storing water in its large root system and rationing it out on an as needed basis. Pinyon pine has a symbiotic relationship with pinyon jays and Clark's nutcrackers, among other birds. The birds gather, store, and feed on the tree's seeds (known as pine nuts). Some of these foraged seeds don't get consumed and instead sprout into new trees. Each party in this exchange contributes to help the other survive.

Big sagebrush, rubber rabbitbrush, Utah serviceberry, and occasional Indian paintbrush adorn the sandy trailside in some stretches. In late spring or early summer some patches of the desert floor are colored purple with hints of silver by the small blooms of woollypod milkvetch; meanwhile, sprightly red or pink sprigs of Bryce Canyon paintbrush aren't uncommon in this driest of understories. Some other plants you may spy here include creeping barberry, elkweed, and Arizona thistle. The red-ochre dominated color palette contributes to the otherworldly vibe here in the seeming maze at the bottom of the canyon.

Clockwise, from top left: Woollypod milkvetch is one of the many colorful wildflowers dressing up the trailside on the way to the Queen's Garden.

Thor's Hammer is one of the iconic hoodoos at Bryce that's known around the world.

Creeping barberry is a hardy native ground cover that can survive in harsh conditions by spreading through underground stems.

Living among the relative floral splendor of the canyon floor is a coterie of smaller fauna you will not likely encounter, as they tend to scamper away long before you might know they are there. These include tiger salamanders, desert striped whipsnakes, common side-blotched lizards, and short-horned lizards, not to mention at least a half dozen different rodent species. Also, Great Basin rattlesnakes lurk in shady spots on the canyon floor, so keep an ear out for their trademark rattle sound—meaning you might be getting too close—and watch where you step.

After spending some quality time in the Queen's Garden, head for the Navajo Loop, which leads back up to the rim near Sunset Point in less than a mile. You'll need to choose which side of the Navajo Loop to take back up to the rim: Wall Street features a slot canyon, while Two Bridges takes you past two natural bridges and right by Thor's Hammer,

◂ It should be no surprise to find the occasional quaking aspen, the most widely distributed tree species in North America, in Bryce Canyon.

another iconic hoodoo often used as a symbol for Bryce Canyon National Park. (The Wall Street side is often closed for bad weather or rockslides, in which case Two Bridges will be the only option.)

Either way, it's a steep climb featuring several switchbacks and gaining more than 500 feet in elevation over just 0.7 mile. Take your time, rest a lot, and make sure you have saved most of your water for this part of the hike—you'll need it. While you may be cursing your way back up to the rim, you'll be so glad you did it when you get there. And you'll have learned a thing or two along the way about the wonders of Mother Nature.

BRYCE CANYON NATIONAL PARK

BRISTLECONE LOOP

Highest elevation section of Bryce features bristlecone pines and views south over Grand Staircase of the Escalante

DIFFICULTY
Easy

LOCATION
Rainbow Point, southern Bryce Canyon

LENGTH
1 mile

WHEELCHAIR ACCESSIBLE
No

PETS ALLOWED
No

And now for something different: the Bristlecone Loop gets you out into the highest section of Bryce National Park, where rare Great Basin bristlecone pine trees are the main attraction instead of red rock hoodoos (although you'll be sure to see a few of those as well). The 1-mile loop trail tops out at just over 9000 feet in elevation, connecting Rainbow and Yovimpa Points while skirting the cliff's edge with views of Bryce Canyon in one direction and the Grand Staircase of the Escalante in the other.

Follow Bryce's 18-mile Scenic Drive south to its terminus at the parking lot for Rainbow Point. Check out the Rainbow Point overlook and get a glimpse of Bryce's amphitheater from this most southerly of perspectives, then pick up the Bristlecone Loop Trail as it heads south along the edge of the canyon for additional hoodoo views. After about 0.2 mile the trail cuts into the woods, with Douglas fir, white fir, and blue spruce trees making for a nice change from the ponderosa pines that dominate in the lower elevations elsewhere around Bryce. Greenleaf manzanita and creeping barberry are among the ground covers making a nice living at ankle height.

Above, from left: Douglas firs are among the tree species found only in this southerly, highest elevation section of Bryce Canyon National Park.

Bryce Canyon is at the eastern edge of the bristlecone pine tree's range, which extends from California's Eastern Sierra across Nevada's highlands and into western Utah.

Much more of a classically forested environment than the rest of Bryce Canyon National Park, wildlife abounds in the trees here. Common ravens and Steller's jays are frequently sighted around these parts, while patient birders may have the luck of seeing a dusky grouse, a downy woodpecker, or a northern pygmy owl. As for mammals, Uinta chipmunks, cliff chipmunks, and rock squirrels are regulars, while mule deer are frequently seen browsing their way through.

Keep walking and within another 0.3 mile the trail leads out onto a point with great views past Bryce Canyon National Park's border and out onto the Grand Staircase of the Escalante spreading out over some 2900 square miles to the southeast. Geologist Clarence Dutton named the region the Grand Staircase in describing the sequence of sedimentary rock layers that descend in elevation from Bryce through the Grand Staircase–Escalante National Monument and Zion National Park into the Grand Canyon.

Bristlecone pine trees, named for the small purple brush-like female cones they produce early in their life cycle, cling to the edge of the cliff and pop up among the other trees of the forest near the trail. These tough, slow-growing trees, with dense, resinous wood that doesn't rot but instead erodes in the elements into sculptured and sanded shapes, live upwards of 1800 years hereabouts. Indeed, bristlecones are known to be the longest living nonclonal organisms on the planet—some specimens in California's High Sierra have made it past their 5000th birthdays. (The only living things older than bristlecone pines are clonal trees like quaking aspen, which reproduce asexually from a common shared root system; the 100-plus acre Pando aspen grove 70 miles north of Bryce near Fish Lake, Utah, consists of about 40,000 "trees" all growing out of still-living clonal roots dating back some 80,000 years.)

Biologists worry that these old bristlecones, while some of the longest lasting of all the trees alive today, may not have long for this world, given sudden habitat shifts due to the rapid onset of global warming and the species' intrinsically slow rate of reproduction coupled with a lack of suitable alternative habitats. The International Union for Conservation of Nature (IUCN) added bristlecone pines to its global "Red List" of endangered species in 1998. That said, the trees seem to be holding on just fine for now, with many of their largest subpopulations within national parks and other public lands where cutting or culling them is prohibited—or in such inaccessible, inhospitable mountain

Reminders of periodic forest fires dot the landscape in this view to the south through the trees and over the Grand Staircase. ▾

◂ While Bryce is known more for hoodoos than arches, Natural Bridge, an arch formed in a sandstone fin toward the southern end of Bryce Canyon, is an exception well worth the pullout along the park's Scenic Drive on the way to or from Rainbow and Yovimpa points.

highlands that the long arm of human development can't reach them. Nevertheless, it will be interesting to see whether increasingly bad symptoms of climate change push the trees over the edge to extinction anyway.

Once you're done looking out onto the Grand Staircase, keep moving along the trail, which cuts back into the woods on its way to the beginning of the loop at the parking lot in another half mile. If it weren't for the canyon views to the north, you might not even know you're in Bryce given how dramatically different the flora here is from the rest of the park. And consider yourself lucky to see some bristlecone pines—they only exist in a few remote spots around the Great Basin—while you still can.

BRYCE CANYON NATIONAL PARK

MOSSY CAVE

Streamside hike to a mossy cave and picturesque waterfall grotto

DIFFICULTY
Easy

LOCATION
Northern Bryce Canyon

LENGTH
0.9 mile

WHEELCHAIR ACCESSIBLE
No

PETS ALLOWED
No

The Mossy Cave section of Bryce Canyon National Park has an oasis-like feeling given its profusion of floral diversity amid the otherwise arid red rock surroundings. The 0.8-mile round-trip hike is easy enough for anyone to handle, and if it's a hot summer day, cooling your feet in Tropic Ditch is a great way to beat the heat.

To get there from the main entrance of Bryce Canyon National Park, drive north on Utah State Route 63 (UT-63) and then hook a right on State Route 12 (UT-12). Anywhere near this junction is a good place to stay alert for Utah prairie dogs. These cute little furballs aren't dogs at all, of course, but are actually pudgy rodents measuring about a foot long and sporting mixed black-brown-and-reddish-brown coats, short white-tipped tails, and black stripes above their eyes that look like eyebrows.

They burrow out elaborate underground "towns" where the entire society resides. If you get too close, you'll hear one or more of them "bark" to warn the others of your presence. While they aren't too scared of humans, you'll hear a racket from them if a raptor is doing an aerial survey or a coyote or rattlesnake is lurking on the outskirts of "town."

Prior to white settlement, Utah prairie dog towns could cover several square miles and contain millions of residents. But these days the population numbers of this endemic species have plummeted thanks to a decades-long effort by local farmers to eradicate them by leaving out poisoned grain.

To counter this decline, Utah prairie dogs were added to the federal Endangered Species List in 1973, and several individuals were reintroduced into Bryce Canyon National

Opposite, clockwise from top: You can walk right underneath the Tropic Ditch waterfall at the far end of the Mossy Cave hike.

Millions of Utah prairie dogs used to inhabit massive "towns" in and around Bryce but nowadays only about 600 of the cute and pudgy rodents make their home here.

Western blue virginsbower dresses up the landscape with a pop of purple.

Park the following year. Those moves likely staved off extinction for the species and have helped them rebound somewhat. More recently, a flea-borne plague has wreaked havoc on prairie dogs' population numbers. Despite these challenges, some 600 or so individuals now reside within park borders, and over the last three decades wildlife biologists have trapped and relocated small groups of them to help establish additional viable colonies outside the park.

Whether or not you get to see any prairie dogs, continue on UT-12 to the Mossy Cave parking area—it can accommodate about two dozen cars—on the west side of the road 3.6 miles east of the junction with UT-63. Pick up the well-marked sandy trail as it cuts through a dense copse of ponderosa pines and continues west through the desert landscape.

If you've already been in the main section of Bryce Canyon National Park, you may be shocked by how much greenery is all around you here. The dominant trees in this lower elevation section are pinyon pines and Utah junipers, but walk a few steps and you're likely to encounter something different—an alderleaf mountain mahogany, a Gambel oak, a single-leaf pinyon, a quaking aspen, or a water birch (with its handsome maroon bark)—along with plenty of ponderosa pines, some blackened from wildfires in previous years.

Utah serviceberry is bushy and stands 6 feet tall. Greenleaf manzanita and narrowleaf yucca pick their spots in the sandy red rock loam the trail bisects. Arizona thistle, rubber rabbitbrush, Canadian lousewort, and Idaho fescue make cameo appearances along the trail and up the adjacent hillsides. Occasional red sprigs of Wyoming paintbrush, the violet bell-shaped flowers of western blue virginsbower, and the star-shaped yellow rosettes of spearleaf stonecrop add some color pop to the otherwise ochre and green landscape.

Utah serviceberry's spindly branches sport big five-petaled white flowers in late spring. ▾

The oasis-like setting attracts lots of wildlife. Spotted towhees and pinyon jays are among the bird species often heard and sometimes seen around here. Uinta

The diverted river water in Tropic Ditch helps make the Mossy Cave area especially oasis-like.

▲ Water birch trees stand sentry at the entrance to Mossy Cave.

chipmunks could be outgoing in their search for handouts, so keep your snacks near and don't be part of the problem—feeding wildlife reduces their ability to survive on their own. If you thought you saw something darting under a rock, it was probably a greater short-horned lizard. These 3- to 4-inch-long reptiles with small, pointed scales around their heads and upper bodies blend in well with the red rock environment given their own rust-pink and black coloration and shale-like appearance.

After about .3 miles, go left at the junction and follow the trail another 300 feet to a dead-end with views up to and under the overhanging ledge that forms Mossy Cave, which is actually more of a large overhanging alcove than a true cave. The "cave" was formed as a result of slightly acidic groundwater seeping through a layer of hard limestone and eroding the underlying softer layers of rock. In winter, these drips become icicles hanging down; by late spring, the moisture down under creates such a damp environment that green moss grows below on the back wall of the cave. A fence prevents visitors from going underneath the overhang and disturbing the otherwise fragile and slippery environment inside.

When you've gotten your fill of Mossy Cave, retrace your steps back down to the trail junction and follow it the other way for another .1 mile as it traces the edge of Tropic Ditch, a man-made waterway created by pioneers in the 1890s to siphon water off of the East Fork of the Sevier River over the cliffs of Bryce Canyon and into the so-called Tropic Valley nearby—a drop of some 1500 feet over a 10-mile run—where enterprising Mormon pioneers used it to irrigate their orchards. Nowadays this riparian corridor is home to diverse plant life, including willow, Nootka rose, and bog orchid, with narrowleaf cottonwood trees overseeing occasional sections of the stream.

This end of the trail dead-ends at a little waterfall where Tropic Ditch drops 15 feet over a rocky ledge. It's not often you get to see—and splash under—a waterfall in the middle of a high, dry desert. Although the stream is man-made, the water in it is as natural as it gets and the fact that this irrigation channel was created so long ago makes it look like a natural landscape feature that's always been there. And while this section of Bryce is more florally diverse than other parts of the national park on its own, the extra water flowing through this little valley no doubt contributes to the preponderance of greenery here.

Surrounding this scenic little oasis is an assortment of red rock hoodoos and buttes, reminding you that you are

The eroded red rock sandstone of the Little Windows reminds you that you are still in Bryce Canyon National Park, albeit on its far northern outskirts. ▾

still in Bryce Canyon National Park. Turret Arch and the Little Windows formation just a few hundred feet to the east provide especially nice framing for this serene setting.

When you've admired the views near and far for long enough, turn around, head back to the junction, turn left, and within another .3 mile you'll be back at the parking lot. While this hike to Mossy Cave and Tropic Ditch waterfall might not be the Bryce experience the majority of visitors get, it's well worth the stop and short hike to get a flavor of the range of biodiversity within this relatively small national park.

ZION NATIONAL PARK

EMERALD POOLS

Classic Zion side canyon hike through pinyon-juniper woodland showcases waterfall-fed gorges

DIFFICULTY
Easy

LOCATION
Zion Canyon

LENGTH
1.4 to 3 miles

WHEELCHAIR ACCESSIBLE
No

PETS ALLOWED
No

This out-and-back hike to the Emerald Pools is a classic Zion experience showcasing lush waterfall-fed gorges and natural pools framed by towering red rock cliffs.

Pick up the trail outside of the Zion Lodge (shuttle stop 5) and cross over the Virgin River on a footbridge. The trail, which is paved but rough all the way to Lower Emerald Pool, meanders along the riverside for approximately 0.3 mile. This verdant riparian zone is awash with a wide range of flora you could almost forget you are in the arid Southwest as you stroll along this oasis-like path.

The pinyon-juniper woodland ecosystem you are traversing—one of five different general ecosystem types at Zion National Park—is named for the dominant tree species here, single-leaf pinyon pines and Utah junipers. Indeed, pinyon-juniper woodlands are common across canyon country, comprising some fifteen percent of the landscapes and a majority of the woodlands of the Four Corners region and providing a wide range of ecosystem services—wildlife habitat, vegetative cover for watershed protection, pinyon nuts for wildlife (and humans) and fuel wood—to the region's diverse populations of flora and fauna.

◂ Zion's Emerald Pools reflect a sense of tranquility, not to mention the surrounding red rock peaks.

Of course, pinyon pines and junipers aren't the only trees around. Closer to the river, Fremont cottonwoods splay out, catching light and moisture. Ascending higher, singleleaf ash and Utah serviceberry make cameos in the shrub layer. An occasional ponderosa pine, complete with vanilla-smelling jigsaw-style bark, stands erect in the forest. Bigtooth maples grow upwards of 45 feet tall and are a common deciduous tree in these parts—their leaves turn bright red and gold in fall. And the contorted branches of an alderleaf mountain mahogany—not a mahogany at all but a member of the rose family and native to this part of the world—remind some visitors of the type of tree they would see on the African savannah.

Watch where you step if you venture off-trail as cacti abound in these lowlands. It's hard to miss the beavertail prickly pear cactus that makes itself at home in these parts, so named for its big, green, spiny, overlapping pads, which are actually a modified, water-conserving form of stem. The spines across the surface of these pads deter interlopers from feeding on the plant's leaves or drinking its reserves of water. That said, some animals—jackrabbits, prairie dogs, javelinas, rodents, bats, iguanas, and coyotes—have evolved adaptations that allow them to partake of the prickly pear's juicy offerings without punishment. In late spring and early summer, the pear-shaped rose-purple flower of the beavertail blooms to the delight of the bees and beetles that feed on the nectar and as such help spread the plant's pollen.

Less common but also fairly widespread here and throughout similar elevations in Zion is the claret cup cactus. Each claret cup plant is composed of dozens of individual green stems tightly grouped into a cluster. In early spring, waxy scarlet-colored blooms, chiefly pollinated by hummingbirds, emerge.

Of course, cacti aren't the only ones sporting blooms in Zion's desert spring. There's a whole lot of herbaceous extravagance going on as well. Keep an eye out for four-wing saltbush, with dozens of little green heart-shaped leaves crowding every stalk. Another trailside bloom you might encounter is sand sagebrush, which looks like Medusa's head or hair in a silver-mint green shade. Little dainty Nuttall's gilias bloom in late spring with floppy white petals surrounding yellow stigmas. Zion shooting-stars flower with distinctive magenta, white, and yellow petals that form the shape of a star. Firecracker penstemons can't be missed with their bright orange-red tubular blooms, which are especially attractive to hummingbirds. And desert globemallow, which grows in wand-like clusters near the tips of skinny erect stems and

Firecracker penstemons wave at passing hummingbirds looking to draw them in for some nectar. ▾

sports apricot-orange flowers punctuated by yellow stigmas, are a key nutrient source for bees and other pollinators.

One particular bee species, the globemallow bee, has evolved to feed exclusively on the nectar of flowers of globemallow plants in a symbiotic relationship where the insect takes the nectar it needs for sustenance but leaves pollen dust—which contains a plant's male sex cells—that the host plant uses for seed propagation.

Of course, the globemallow bee is far from the only pollinator buzzing around Zion: more than 250 different species of bees inhabit the nectar-rich valley of the Virgin River and surrounding Zion lands. Perhaps the most common bee here, as practically everywhere across the Lower 48, is the world's most economically important and intensively studied insect, the honeybee. These non-native stingers were first introduced to the New World by Spanish settlers in the 1500s and later to Utah by Mormons in the 1840s. The feral descendants of these initially domesticated colonies play a large role in pollinating plants (and crops) coast to coast to this day. In fact, researchers estimate that honeybees are responsible for pollinating 80 percent of all flowering plants across the United States. That's why mysterious sporadic declines in honeybee populations in recent decades have worried not only environmentalists and biologists, but farmers, food distributors and retailers, and economists as well.

Here at Zion, honeybees build colonies in just about any alcove, rock crevice, or cave that isn't already inhabited. Predators of the bees or their stores of honey—or ill-fated humans who step in the wrong place—should be prepared to be mobbed and stung repeatedly, with each individual defender bee sacrificing its own life, leaving its stinger embedded in the victim. And while there may be a lot of fear in the Southwest about rattlesnakes, honeybees are statistically the most dangerous wildlife in the U.S., with more direct kills of humans than any other animal.

Soon enough, the trail turns west, leaving the riverside and heading into Heaps Canyon, where erosion has worked its magic over the eons, turning a small fissure in the 180 million-year-old sandstone into a narrow slot canyon that eventually opens up and empties out into Zion's main canyon where you are now. As you gradually ascend, look for views back to the Virgin River and the surrounding

▲ A mule deer skirts an abundant patch of beavertail prickly pear cacti.

sandstone cliffs rising so dramatically from the canyon floor. As you get deeper into the forest and further from the river, the sweet high, sporadic sound of birdsong slowly eclipses the swoosh of rushing water. Yellow warblers, one of the most widespread and adaptable of all songbird species, are frequently singers in this chorus. Look for the bird's small yellow body flitting through the surrounding trees. Some 291 different bird species live in or pass through Zion; the yellow warbler is one of the 100-plus species that actually breed within park boundaries, making them among Zion's truly native birds.

Continue to climb gradually and after half a mile of hiking you'll enter the red rock alcove housing Lower Emerald Pool, a serene, green-tinged pond reflecting the surrounding cliffs. If it's spring or early summer, you'll likely be treated to the visual delight of veils of water cascading over the canyon walls you are crossing under. This wispy but nevertheless powerful waterfall jumps the very cliff you are hiking below, so be prepared to get wet from the spray, especially if the wind is blowing. A sturdy metal handrail can be helpful as the trail often gets muddy along this section.

If a short and easy hike to a beautiful destination like Lower Emerald Pool is all you came for, you can turn around and retrace your steps back to the trailhead near Zion

Lodge—a respectable 1.2-mile round-trip hike. But if you want to get more steps in and get your heart pounding a bit—not to mention lose most of the crowds—consider moving higher and deeper into Heaps Canyon via the well-marked trail to Middle Emerald Pool and Upper Emerald Pool.

If you do go onward and upward, the trail gets more difficult as the elevation grade steepens. Continue up from the Lower Pool as the trail passes through some rocky terrain and skirts several huge "glacial erratic" boulders—large rocks transported and deposited by glaciers, often far from their original location.. The well-maintained trail features several sections of stairsteps that make the climbing a bit easier, as well as some squeezing through tight slots between red rock fins. Within another 0.3 mile, you'll arrive at Middle Emerald Pool, where the two streams that shower Lower Emerald Pool just below merge into one. This middle pool is slightly smaller than Lower Emerald but arguably even more tranquil, perhaps in part because most of the crowds turned back before they ever got here.

If it's mating season, listen for the croaks and bellows of canyon tree frogs copulating in shallow pools near the trailside. If you are lucky enough to hear this loud and raucous noise, follow the sound to its source and chances are you'll be able to see the tree frogs in action with your own two eyes. The fact that these amphibians are masters of camouflage—they can shift the color of their skin depending on their surroundings—and they are primarily nocturnal means you should feel privileged if you get to see them in the middle of the day. But apparently priorities like keeping a low profile and staying out of sight go out the window during the late spring mating season.

Now that you've made it to Middle Emerald Pool, assess your energy level to decide whether to turn around, making for a 2.2-mile out-and-back hike—or keep ascending to check out Upper Emerald Pool, which would add another (steep) 0.75 mile to your total hiking mileage. While this last push up into Heaps Canyon is

Canyon tree frogs like the untrammeled sidewash near the trail junction to Middle Emerald Falls. ▾

▲ There are a few tight squeezes along the way to Upper Emerald Falls, but the National Park Service does everything it can to keep the trail passable.

a bit of a thigh-burner, no one seems to regret making the extra effort.

Indeed, there is nary a sight in all of Zion as intimate yet grandiose as this view of the shallow and green Upper Emerald Pool, which sits at the base of an imposing 300-foot-tall red rock cliff. In spring and early summer, a long, horse-tailing waterfall showers down at the far end of the pool. Find a boulder where you can sit and eat a snack or drink some water and take in this temple of nature.

Once you've bathed yourself in the splendor of the scene long enough, retrace your steps back down to the trail junction and hang a left to loop down to a different river crossing after which you can then follow the Grotto Trail on the opposite side of the Virgin River back to your starting point at the Zion Lodge. You've been good and earned a treat, so make your way to the lodge's outdoor beer garden or head inside and grab a prickly pear margarita and a Navajo taco from the Red Rock Grill.

Hiking to Lower Emerald Pool is a wonderful introduction to the natural wonders of Zion National Park. It offers a taste of the park's stunning scenery and is suitable for hikers of all skill levels. Don't forget to savor the breathtaking views and take your time to immerse yourself in the awe-inspiring beauty of this iconic canyon.

ZION NATIONAL PARK

RIVERSIDE WALK

Riverside stroll along the rushing Virgin River surrounded by lush greenery and towering red rock cliffs

DIFFICULTY
Easy

LOCATION
Zion Canyon

LENGTH
1.9 miles

WHEELCHAIR ACCESSIBLE
Partially, the first 0.4 miles

PETS ALLOWED
No

The Riverside Walk is an easy 1.9-mile out-and-back hike that winds along the bottom of Zion Canyon and gets you right up alongside the rushing Virgin River and a wide range of native flora along the way. Towering red rock sandstone cliffs rise along both sides of the river, and songbirds flit in and out of the trees. The mostly flat and paved trail is wheelchair-accessible, and as such is also friendly to small kids, great-grandparents, and anyone in between. This is one trail in Zion that no one should miss.

You can get there by taking the free Zion shuttle to its northern terminus at the Temple of Sinawava (stop 9), where the well-marked Riverside Walk begins alongside the river. It's a great feeling to head north and leave the road and the crowded bus behind; only hikers can access this wilder section of Zion Canyon, so, despite the crowds, you can feel more immersed in nature.

The trail snakes its way along the east bank of the Virgin River, offering many spots to diverge from the pavement and cut out onto the gravelly shoreline where you can dip your toes in the water if you so choose. Strategically placed stone benches here and there along the trail—many shaded in leafy deciduous groves—provide respite for those needing

◂ The Riverside Walk is paved and mostly level, allowing anyone who can walk or roll access to this otherwise wild and pristine canyon.

▸ Velvet ash groves provide shady rest spots along the Riverside Walk.

▲ Whitewater kayakers have no trouble powering their way downstream in the fast-moving waters of the Virgin River.

a breather or a stationary place to contemplate the wonders of nature all around.

Don't sit too long or one of the assertive rock squirrels that call the Riverside Walk home will no doubt approach looking for a handout. While these squirrels may look cute and seem friendly, feeding them human food is a bad idea as they cannot digest everything we can and they lose their ability to fend for themselves from the bounty of Mother Nature. Of course, lots of other wildlife frequent this part of Zion—mule deer, Rocky Mountain elk, desert bighorn sheep, mountain lions, bobcats, badgers, marmots, ringtails, Mexican spotted owls, and the endemic Zion snail, to name a few—but many are nocturnal and none are as friendly as the overserved rock squirrels.

Fremont cottonwood trees, which thrive when they have a constant water source like here along the riverside, sprawl out big and wide, topping out at about 90 feet tall with canopy spreads almost as wide thanks to long, stout overhanging branches. In midspring the tree produces and eventually

drops hundreds of catkins—6-inch-long skinny clusters of white, downy seed-bearing flowers that break free and drift in the air column, lending the valley a white-veiled mystical atmosphere that only adds to the scene's already otherworldly beauty. Sunlight filters through their leaf canopies, shading sporadic stretches of river below, effectively creating different riparian and aquatic microclimates, which helps maintain biodiversity in the wider ecosystem.

The trees are also an important structural element of Zion's landscape, stabilizing stream banks up and down the course of the Virgin River and its tributaries while dropping lots of woody debris into the watercourse below to help provide more diverse habitat for fish. Healthy Fremonts in prime spots can expect to live upwards of 120 years, although most of their growing—a whopping 10 to 20 feet a year—goes on during their first few decades.

Of course, these trees are beloved by not only humans but wildlife as well. American beavers rely on them as a primary source for building materials for their dams and lodges—look for gnawed-off tree limbs, a sure sign that beavers have been busy there—but also as a food source. The nutrient-filled cambium, the sappy layer of lifeblood between a tree's trunk and bark, is a staple energy source in the beaver's diet. Mule deer and desert cottontail rabbits also munch on cottonwood leaves, and many birds use the trees for roosting and nesting.

Sadly, Zion's cottonwoods are not regenerating at a pace quickly enough to stave off their eventual die-off in Zion Canyon. The problem started when well-meaning engineers designed and implemented a system of levees in the 1930s to protect the then-new Zion Canyon Scenic Road and prevent Zion Lodge from being inundated every spring with floodwaters.

But it turns out that altering the natural flow of the Virgin River through Zion Canyon and eliminating the flooding of certain areas along the way was the beginning of the end of the cottonwoods' run here. Before the levees, some of the cottonwoods' downy airborne seeds would land along sections of the riparian zone that were still saturated with floodwaters, making for a perfect environment in which to take root. Without flooded stream banks up and down the river's course through the canyon, cottonwood seeds had a much harder time germinating.

Above, from left: A rotund rock squirrel looks to have been well-fed by previous human passersby.

Gambel oaks are notable for reproducing in two different ways. Like any other oak, they fruit out in fall by producing and dropping acorns, each containing the seed for a new tree. But they also spread from root sprouts that grow from networks of underground structures called lignotubers, so it's not uncommon to see several of them clustered together.

When the National Park Service finally figured out the problem, they proceeded with efforts to replant cottonwoods throughout potentially promising locations in the canyon, but these saplings never seemed to make it to maturity. The problem this time around was the out-of-control population of mule deer browsing every fresh young shoot in the canyon. Mountain lions have historically been the chief predator of mule deer in this part of the world, but the big cats are leery of humans, and as such tend to avoid crowded Zion Canyon, giving the deer free rein. While the current generation of essentially now elderly cottonwoods in Zion seem to be healthy enough, the lack of a new generation is what worries those who love nature and natural beauty. When the cottonwoods here today die off over the next three to four decades, there may not be any to replace them—which makes now a particularly good time to visit Zion.

While the Fremont cottonwood is Zion's most iconic plant species, nature lovers will notice many other charismatic flora along the way. Box elders, bigtooth maples, Utah junipers, single-leaf ashes, velvet ashes, ponderosa pines, and Gambel oaks also show up in droves in and around the Virgin River valley.

Spring is a great time of year to visit Zion if you like wildflowers, and the lush riparian zone along the Riverside Walk is prime real estate for colorful and aromatic blooms. One you can't miss if you time your visit right is the 3-plus-foot-tall, rosy-smelling Palmer's penstemon, with purple-veined pale pink blossoms scaling a sturdy central stem buoyed by boat-shaped leaf pairs at the bottom. There's also Zion shooting-star, which features blooms with small bent-back pale purple petals surrounding a core yellow ovule with a protruding cluster of yellow-brown stamens that converge in a point, giving the whole package an arrow-like demeanor. Golden columbine, canyon grape, common dogbane, and jimsonweed are but a few of the other flowers the observant hiker can notice while on the Riverside Walk.

All the while, the sound of the rushing Virgin River provides a pleasant backing track. You might see a whitewater kayaker or two riding the torrent of the river downstream, but there's a lot more action going on underneath the surface. Four native fish species—the flannelmouth sucker, desert sucker, speckled dace, and Virgin spinedace—call this stretch of the Virgin home. The latter, a speckled silver minnow with orange gills, is endemic to (that is, only found in) the Virgin River and its tributaries. But drought, global warming, and overuse of Virgin basin water for human needs have combined to reduce the range of the spinedace by some 60 percent over just a few decades, leading biologists to worry that this unique aquatic species was headed for extinction. A consortium of interested public entities and conservation groups stepped in and created a management plan in 1995 to help restore spinedace habitat along the course of the Virgin River through Zion. Cut to the present and spinedace are now back in 90 percent of their historical range thanks to the plan in what all parties consider a conservation success story.

After an easy mile, the paved Riverside Walk comes to an end. Unless you are undertaking the canyoneering adventure of "hiking" the Narrows—a 3.6-mile partially submerged stretch of Zion Canyon extending north that takes all day to hike—here is your turnaround point. Enjoy the view to the north where the pavement ends, wish the canyoneers heading that way good luck, and turn around to make your way back to the trailhead at the Temple of Sinawava. You'll no doubt notice different flowers, trees, and vistas on the way back, so take your time and enjoy the experience while you check one of Zion's "must-do" hikes off your bucket list.

ZION NATIONAL PARK

WEEPING ROCK

Sidewall seep oasis where maidenhair ferns and wildflowers dominate on the east side of Zion Canyon

DIFFICULTY
Easy

LOCATION
Zion Canyon

LENGTH
0.3 mile

WHEELCHAIR-ACCESSIBLE
No

PETS ALLOWED
No

Follow this short trail up a verdant hillside on the eastern flank of Zion Canyon where a dripping shelf of Navajo sandstone hangs over an older layer of Kayenta shale, forming a hanging garden where maidenhair ferns and other plants thrive. Along the way you'll cross over a picturesque stream of Weeping Rock's making that helps give the hillside below a lush, wildflower-festooned look.

To get there, hop on the Zion shuttle and get off at Weeping Rock (stop 7). Follow the crowd along the well-marked, paved trail that first cuts over a small footbridge over Weeping Rock's stream before turning and heading uphill.

The short hike is paved throughout, although too steep for wheelchairs. You'll pass through a "sloping swamp" featuring some of the lushest foliage you'll see in Zion thanks to the drip irrigation from above. If the sun is out, you'll appreciate the shade of a mature box elder tree with a big, wide deciduous canopy of semitranslucent green leaves that turn a brilliant yellow in fall. This unique species of maple can get as big as 80 feet tall over a lifespan of up to 75 years. Unlike other maples, box elders are strictly

◂ This big old box elder tree provides some shade for hikers making their way up the exposed hillside to Weeping Rock.

▸ A bigtooth maple tree thrives in a lush opening just off the trail to Weeping Rock.

dioecious, meaning separate neighboring male and female trees are needed for reproduction to occur. (Most maples are monoecious, meaning they have separate male and female flowers on the same tree.)

Bigtooth maples, a little cousin to the bigger box elders, have also found a nice home here on this hillside. This tree grows to about 50 feet tall over an 80-year lifespan. Its leaves are a darker green and turn red and orange in October around these parts. Both of these trees thrive in the sunlight and moisture here on this exposed and naturally irrigated hillside. Their relatively deep roots help stabilize the often-saturated hillside, while their branches, cavities, and bark provide lots of roosting terrain and nesting habitat for a wide range of insects and birds.

While the hillside here is beautiful year-round, it's springtime when it really comes alive with wildflower blooms—and the pollinators that love them. Keep an eye out for hairy false goldenaster, which features small clusters of sprawling yellow flowers with gray-green leaves. Meanwhile, cardinal monkeyflowers, with spreading orange-red flowers and toothed downy leaves, stretch to 3 feet tall in some instances. Another showy bloom you may encounter here is golden columbine, which thrives in moist canyon seeps like the one you are hiking through. Moths, butterflies, and bees are all attracted to this beauty, making the flower a true Grand Central Station of pollination. If you're lucky you'll find some canyon grapes, an edible purple wild grape that grows on deciduous vines and is a favorite snack for birds, rodents, and even passing humans. Sand sagebrush fills in the gaps with its feathery, silver-blue foliage while lending a sweetly pungent aroma to the air.

While the hike isn't particularly long nor particularly steep, getting your steps in this way sure beats getting them by walking around the shopping mall back home. Cresting the high point in the trail, you'll be under the overhang of Weeping Rock. A healthy-looking population of southern maidenhair ferns has made the place their home, drinking in the misty moisture as water seeps through 2000 feet of Navajo red rock sandstone from a depression up top known as Echo Canyon—and drips below onto the supporting Kayenta shale, which constitutes the prevalent base layer at this elevation in the canyon.

▲ Looking down canyon from Weeping Rock yields an epic view of the Great White Throne and surrounding red rock cliffs anchored by the rolling green canopy of Fremont cottonwood trees along the banks of the Virgin River.

▲ Zion shooting-stars bloom into lavender and yellow darts across the park in spring.

▲ There is all the sunlight and moisture a southern maidenhair fern could want under the misty ledge of Weeping Rock.

While it's cozy but a little wet in this tucked away alcove, the views outward can't be beat. Look south—otherwise known as "down canyon"—towards a vista featuring the Great White Throne, an iconic Zion natural monolith capped with white Navajo sandstone that can be seen from most locations along the park's Scenic Road due to its prominent spot midvalley. The surrounding red rock cliffs are flanked by green canopies of Fremont cottonwoods, ponderosa pines, and a relatively diverse assortment of other trees and plants given the arid setting.

If you see a fast bird swooping by, it's probably a white-throated swift. These black-and-white speedsters (named "swift" because they fly so fast) live on the cliffside and feed "on the wing" on small insects flying through the air. Violet-green swallows also operate under a similar MO, living in the cliffs and foraging for their dinners while aloft. Another bird to keep an eye (or ear) out for is the white-breasted nuthatch; these stout little white-gray-black songbirds are famous for being able to walk down tree trunks with their heads aimed straight down.

When the chill under the dripping ledge has gotten to you, it's time to turn around and head back down. While Weeping Rock may not be the most dramatic setting in all of Zion, you won't regret making the short hike to this verdant cliffside nook, which may indeed be one of Zion's most biodiverse little corners.

ZION NATIONAL PARK

GROTTO TRAIL

Stroll through a boulder-filled landscape punctuated by cottonwoods and cacti following the curves of the nearby Virgin River

DIFFICULTY
Easy

LOCATION
Zion Canyon

LENGTH
1.2 miles

WHEELCHAIR ACCESSIBLE
No

PETS ALLOWED
No

One of the most popular and easy-to-access nature walks in all of Zion, the Grotto Trail is a great introduction to what makes this national park so special. Smack dab in the middle of Zion, the half-mile valley floor jaunt winds through rock-laden landscapes dressed up with cottonwoods and cacti, and it features vistas of towering Navajo sandstone cliffs and the rushing steel-green Virgin River. Many hikers use the Grotto Trail as a warm-up and connector trail for longer hikes around Zion, while others consider the mile-long out-and-back hike plenty of exercise for the day.

Most people hike the Grotto Trail from south to north (starting at Zion Lodge) and then retrace their steps, but you can do it either way—or even one way, hopping on the shuttle after that to go to another destination. Look for the trailhead near the north end of the Zion Lodge's shuttle pickup area (stop 5). The predominantly concrete and sandy trail is mostly flat and easily navigable but not necessarily wheelchair accessible. This first part of the Grotto Trail follows the course of the original one-lane dirt road through Zion Canyon built in 1916, which was eventually

▲ Box elder trees provide lots of shade along the flat and wide Grotto Trail.

replaced by the Zion Canyon Scenic Drive the shuttle buses traverse today.

Leaving the hubbub of the scene around Zion Lodge behind you, walk north through a pleasant wooded meadow with box elders, bigtooth maples, Gambel oaks, Utah junipers, and Fremont cottonwoods lining the trailside. The cottony debris from the latter tree—actually the cottonwood's airborne seeds dispersing themselves—can clog the air column in Zion Canyon during spring. As you hike, keep your eyes peeled for various rock outcroppings harboring beavertail prickly pear cacti and even a few of its more elusive cousin, the claret cup.

You can tell the claret cups by their funnel-shaped scarlet blooms in spring. These are "mounding" cacti, meaning they form bulbous piles of a few or many spherical stems that are densely covered in spines and woolly in appearance. Stringy pink stamens at the center of the flower's corolla attract hummingbirds to the cactus's thick nectar chamber.

Black-chinned hummingbirds are the most common hummers around Zion, with dull metallic green heads and wings; the males are distinguished by hints of iridescent purple at the base of their otherwise black throats. Also keep an eye out for broad-tailed hummingbirds, which sport stunning iridescent green heads and wings, with the males

▸ Claret cup cacti's cuplike scarlet blooms come out in spring.

▸ Huge Navajo sandstone boulders have come loose from the cliffs above and ended up on the valley floor.

differentiated by a magenta throat patch. Every spring, both of these species helicopter in, build nests, and commence breeding here—probably not too far from where you are standing on the Grotto Trail, given their nesting preference for low-lying, mostly horizontal cottonwood branches hanging over the Virgin River. Given this abundance of habitat and the profusion of spring wildflower blooms, hummingbirds love Zion Canyon—and chances are decent you'll experience one or two of them here if you are quiet and observant.

Songbirds are also omnipresent in this part of Zion. If you listen closely, you are likely to hear the "sweet, sweet, sweet, I'm so sweet" chirping pattern of yellow warblers, or the churr, chatter, and rattle of house wrens warning of big predators (like you) nearby. American dippers, western bluebirds, spotted towhees, and American robins are among the other songbirds frequently seen or heard along the Grotto Trail.

And if you happen to see a group of 3-foot-tall gangly birds doing a funky walk somewhere near the trail, say hello to Zion's Rio Grande wild turkeys. While fossil records show evidence of wild turkeys around these parts in prehistoric times, the birds hadn't been present in and around Zion for centuries by the time the national park was established in 1919. Around then, wildlife managers began several failed attempts to relocate wild turkeys from other parts of the country to this part of Utah.

It wasn't until the 1980s when a transfer of several hundred Rio Grande wild turkeys native to the central plains started successfully reproducing in and around verdant Zion Canyon. Nowadays some 20,000 wild turkeys call greater Zion home. They especially like the flats around the Virgin River and as such are often seen crossing over the Grotto Trail. While you might have thought of turkeys as flightless birds, it's only the overstuffed farm-raised ones sold as food for Thanksgiving dinner (or your lunch sandwich) that can't take flight because they are too heavy. Their wild cousins, like those wandering near the Grotto Trail, weigh half as much and can indeed take flight, albeit for short distances. To wit, every evening Zion's turkeys fly up into the surrounding Fremont cottonwood boughs to roost for the night.

After about a quarter mile of walking, the trail starts to parallel Zion Park Scenic Drive, and although there is some greenery as a buffer, don't be alarmed by the sound of the Zion shuttle rumbling by on its way between stops for Zion Lodge and the Grotto. You had a good run getting away from the trappings of civilization, but it can't last forever.

Speaking of the Grotto, keep walking north and soon enough you'll be at its picnic area. The Grotto was one of several smaller campgrounds in the park until the 1960s when the National Park Service consolidated campers at Watchman Campground and South Campground. At that point, they also converted the Grotto to the picnic area it is today, with a rudimentary bathroom and water station as

Above, from left: Wild turkeys, reintroduced to the region in the 1980s, may be the most commonly seen bird in Zion National Park these days.

Utah juniper's chalky white berries are edible but humans find them too tart to enjoy; that said, they are a staple in the diets of jackrabbits, coyotes, and a variety of birds.

well as an array of picnic tables scattered throughout the huge boulders that give the spot its name.

If you brought a snack or sandwich, grab a table and have a bite. Otherwise, hop on the shuttle (you're right at stop 6 for the Grotto now) or continue hiking elsewhere. If you are continuing on foot, you can turn around and retrace your steps back to Zion Lodge via the same half mile you just traversed and get a different perspective on the short but sweet Grotto Trail. If you're really ambitious, cross over the river to the west and head out on the Kayenta Trail to either the Emerald Pools or Angel's Landing, two of the most iconic hikes in Zion for those looking to put more serious mileage on their boots. No matter which route you choose, you'll no doubt be rewarded with sublime scenery and a deeper understanding of the very nature of Zion.

BEYOND ZION NATIONAL PARK

CORAL PINK SAND DUNES

Orange-pink desert red rock sand dunes shapeshift with the passing wind

	DIFFICULTY Easy to moderate
LOCATION 20 miles southeast of Zion	LENGTH 0.25 mi. or more
WHEELCHAIR-ACCESSIBLE Yes, to Observation Deck	PETS ALLOWED Yes

While not within the limits of Zion National Park, the otherworldly landscape at Coral Pink Sand Dunes State Park—where orange-pink sand dunes constantly shift and reform themselves with the passing wind as an odd assortment of plants and animals hang on for dear life—is well worth the short detour if you are driving between Zion and points south.

From U.S. Route 89 (US-89) west of Kanab, Utah, take the well-marked turnoff onto Sand Dune Road, and follow it west to the state park entrance. Check in at the drive-through window at the visitor center and pay your day use fee ($10) for free rein of the park. Continue straight and turn right, following the park road for approximately another 500 feet to the observation deck parking area. This is a great place to start your exploration of the dunes on foot. While the setting is beautiful all day long, try to time your visit during the "golden hour"—an hour before sunset when the low rays of the dropping sun tint the dunes an extra warm red—for the best views and photographs.

Wind your way on the paved path past pinyon pine and Utah juniper trees out to the observation deck, a raised metal platform on the edge of the dunes. There's room for dozens of visitors to get a good overview of the scene, but chances are you'll have the deck all to yourself. Drink in the otherworldly views of the coral-pink sand dunes spread out before you.

This is one of the most unique and dynamic landscapes in all of the Southwest. Persistent southerly winds funnel through a notch between Moquith and Moccasin mountains just to the south of the state park. As the wind passes through the narrow gap, its velocity increases dramatically—a physics principle known as the Venturi effect—to the point where it picks up and carries sand grains from nearby eroding Navajo sandstone cliffs. (The reddish sand gets its color from iron oxides and other minerals in the Navajo sandstone.)

◂ The wind has been depositing Navajo sandstone sand into this basin through the notch between Moquith and Moccasin mountains for more than 10,000 years.

After the wind passes through the notch, its velocity quickly decreases and its passengers—those flying grains of coral-colored sand—are dumped in the open valley below, forming the only major dune field in the entire Four Corners region. The geography of the valley and the frequency of the wind means that these sand grains won't stay put for long once they are initially laid down, moving in sandy coral-colored waves sometimes 60 feet tall.

Once you've gotten a good meta view of the dunes thanks to the observation deck, head on out into the sand on foot. Most people keep their footwear on, but feel free to give it a try barefoot, as the sand feels silky underfoot. (Some dune trekkers swear by wearing socks only on their feet to protect against the heat of the sand but still enjoy the tactile experience.) There aren't trails per se in the constantly shifting sand, but you can follow in others' footsteps if it makes you feel better about not getting lost. Indeed, it can be hard to tell in which direction you're heading when you're down in a swale between 60-foot-tall sand dunes. That said, you can always climb up one side or the other and look for the observation deck if you are anxious about getting back.

Whatever route into the dunes suits you is fine. Beware of off-road vehicles (ORVs) as they are allowed on 90 percent of the dune field. You can usually hear them coming but always keep your wits about you (and leave the headphones or boombox in the car). If you head due east from the observation deck, you will hit the other side of the dunefield within .75 mile. Alternatively, do a circular loop around the dunefield in either direction. However you tackle it, just make sure to bring plenty of water—there is little to no shade out there—and save enough energy to get back.

Given the inhospitable nature of the dunes, with constantly shifting sands burying one another and forming anew, plants are few and far between. That said, the plants that do maintain a presence here are adapted specifically to the setting with physiological strategies that help them survive where others cannot. For instance, rubber rabbitbrush sheds its leaves during drought in order to save water, while Mormon tea has tiny leaves to reduce surface area exposed to the hot and drying sun. Rough mule's ears and fringe-leaf necklacepod have deep taproot systems so they

▸ The thick waxy surface of the Kanab yucca's stiff, sword-shaped leaves helps it retain water.

can draw moisture and sustenance from deep below, and big sandreed, Kanab yucca, and Welsh's milkvetch reproduce vegetatively via a network of underground rhizomes.

As a result of their rhizomatic reproduction, this latter group of plants is typically the first to colonize newly formed dunes here. Welsh's milkvetch, for instance, has rhizomes that penetrate deep below the surface, possibly all the way to the underlying bedrock. As such, several widely spaced milkvetch stems could all belong to one underground plant. Researchers estimate some 20,000 Welsh's milkvetch

Small vernal pools that form at the base of the shifting dunes create their own mini-ecosystems.

stems span the state park's 3700 acres, although no one knows how many (or how few) genetically separate individual rhizomes these visible stalks grow from.

Back in 1987, the U.S. Fish & Wildlife Service listed the species as threatened under the Endangered Species Act (ESA). These protections allowed land managers to cordon off certain sections of the dunescape to ORVs, which tend to tear up young milkvetch shoots. The species has rebounded as a result, even spreading beyond park boundaries onto neighboring Bureau of Land Management lands. While ORVs remain a threat to the plant given their continued presence here, climate change looms larger as a problem for this threatened species. Rising temperatures can lead to premature drying of the plant prior to seed germination. Only time will tell whether Welsh's milkvetch can survive, but for now no one is suggesting removing its protection under the ESA.

If you are here in spring, you'll notice ephemeral vernal pools dotting the low points of the dunescape. These seasonal oases, often fringed with willow, miner's lettuce, stonecrop, and woodland star, serve as magnets for life, begetting small populations of tadpoles, salamanders, and insects. Perhaps the most famous of these small wonders eking out a living in and around the vernal pools is the Coral Pink Sand Dunes tiger beetle, which only occurs here in this unique landscape, and lives its entire life cycle burrowed underground. Researchers have discovered that the population of these endemic beetles rises and falls year to year based on moisture in the terrain. Environmentalists would still like to see them protected under the ESA as well, but the U.S. Fish & Wildlife Service passed on listing the beetle in 2012, citing the fact that its population numbers were linked to weather changes rather than any form of human encroachment. When viewed through the current day's lens, however, maybe it makes sense to revisit protecting the Coral Pink Sand Dunes tiger beetle given the eventual depletion of the vernal pools where they live, as temperatures everywhere rise and our world gets drier.

Of course, there is lots of other wildlife around as well, and thankfully it is less rare. That said, the animals that are successful in making their home here are well adapted to the dry conditions. To wit, desert woodrats and Ord's kangaroo rats are both nocturnal rodents that rest underground during the heat of the day and forage at night for seeds, stems, and dried plant matter. Neither species ever drinks water per se, instead metabolizing all the hydration they need from their food.

Meanwhile, black-tailed jackrabbits—strict herbivores sustaining themselves on grasses, rabbitbrush, and cacti, among other plants—keep from overheating by circulating blood through the skin of their large ears to release body heat as they scurry from bush to bush, worriedly nibbling as they go.

Antelope ground squirrels are no strangers to park visitors. The little chipmunk-like rodents may be cute, but don't give them human food handouts, as it impedes their ability to forage for their own food in the environment. Meanwhile, mule deer, coyotes, kit foxes, mountain lions, and bobcats also spend time in and around the dunescape, but you'll have to be lucky to catch a glimpse of any of them given their wariness of humans. Keep an eye out for tracks in the sand, however.

If you like reptiles (or not), keep your eyes peeled for desert horned lizards, Great Basin collared lizards, and gopher snakes—and watch where you step as you wouldn't want to upset a resting Great Basin rattlesnake. As for birds, western meadowlarks, sage thrashers, Say's phoebes, western bluebirds, chipping sparrows, common ravens, red-tailed hawks, golden eagles, and prairie falcons are among the avian species all making a good living at the dunes. Bald eagles don't nest here but can sometimes be found roosting in the trees at the edge of the dunes in winter.

With no set route through the dunes, take as much time as you want to wander and get acquainted with the coral-pink sand and the flora and fauna that call it home. When you've had your fill, or your shoes are filled with sand, head back toward the observation deck and say goodbye to perhaps the most unique landscape you'll see in all your wandering across Southwest canyon country.

GLEN CANYON
NATIONAL
RECREATION AREA
HANGING
GARDEN
BEEHIVE TRAIL
AND THE
NEW WAVE
LAKE POWELL
KANAB
89
PAGE
NAVAJO
SLOT
CANYONS
BRIGHT
ANGEL
POINT
89A
67
GRAND CANYON
NATIONAL PARK
98
COLORADO
RIVER
CAPE ROYAL
TRAIL
89
BRIGHT ANGEL
TRAIL TO 1.5-MILE
RESTHOUSE
64
SHOSHONE
POINT
SOUTH KAIBAB TRAIL
TO OOH AAH POINT
64
180
FLAGSTAFF
40

ARIZONA

SAN JUAN RIVER

UTAH

ARIZONA

PETRIFIED FOREST NATIONAL PARK

PAINTED DESERT RIM TRAIL

40

BLUE MESA TRAIL

HOLBROOK

180

CRYSTAL FOREST

GIANT LOGS TRAIL

NEW MEXICO

GLEN CANYON NATIONAL RECREATION AREA

HANGING GARDEN

Hike through classic Glen Canyon hot, dry desert to a seep spring oasis under a sandstone ledge

	DIFFICULTY Easy
LOCATION Antelope Point, southern Glen Canyon	LENGTH 1.4 miles
WHEELCHAIR ACCESSIBLE No	PETS ALLOWED Yes

The short hike to the Hanging Garden just outside of Page, Arizona, may be the perfect antidote to the otherwise dry and sandy environment all around you in Glen Canyon National Recreation Area. This veritable oasis of life growing out of a sandstone cliffside is just .75 mile from the trailhead and features a diverse array of flowering plants that attracts lots of wildlife, not to mention human lovers of nature.

To get there, drive north on U.S. Route 89 (US-89) from the city of Page, turn right on Chains Road, and follow it for a quarter mile to the small, well-marked parking area for the Hanging Garden Trail. Pick up the "trail" as it crosses over sandstone slabs—carefully placed stones on both sides keep you on track—and walk north through the sagebrush-dominated scene along the base of a small outcrop. Keep an eye out for prickly pear and barrel cacti, each of which blooms out in beautiful flowers in late spring.

◂ Little rocks demarcate the edge of the "trail" as it heads out across slabs of striated Navajo sandstone on the way to the Hanging Garden.

▾ Rubber rabbitbrush, common throughout Navajo country in northern Arizona, is an important food source for mule deer, pronghorn, and jackrabbits.

If you notice a wee bit of movement out of the corner of your eye, stop and examine the sandstone wall to your right. It may well be a common chuckwalla. These lizards range from 16 to 22 inches long and are typically black, black-and-white banded, or a mottled gray and white, sometimes with subtle rust-colored spots—but they can change from lighter to darker when it's cold to absorb more solar heat. Primarily vegetarians, chuckwallas dine on a range of local leaves, flowers, and fruits, but may occasionally eat insects and insect larvae. They evade predators (birds, snakes) by blending in with their surroundings, and look a little like minidinosaurs. (Their long-forgotten ancestors, real dinosaurs, roamed this region extensively during the Jurassic era approximately

150 million years ago.) If they catch you watching them, they may freeze in place for a minute before darting into a dark crevice in the sandstone.

Another form of wildlife common in these parts that you're unlikely to see by the light of day is the woodrat, a nocturnal white-pink mouselike "pack rat" rodent measuring only 11 to 15 inches long. But you may see their middens. Desert woodrats and the three other woodrat species that call this part of the world home are known for building garbage structures called middens where they discard their used-up leaves, seeds, fruit, sticks, pollen, bones, and other items, marking the resulting heaps with their urine, which serves to fossilize the contents. Biologists can sample these middens and glean information on the dietary habits of woodrats over time. Indeed, some of the middens in this neck of the desert are upwards of 50,000 years old, and as such are treasure troves of data about the changes in plant communities here for eons past. Researchers are using this information to predict future floral patterns given recent temperature shifts from global warming.

Keep moving and at about half a mile in, take a right at the Hanging Garden sign and start winding your way up the flank of the broad sandstone ridge above you. As you make slight gains in elevation, you'll notice more and more greenery.

Trickles of water from a spring up above seep down here, giving a wide range of desert plants the moisture they need to thrive despite the otherwise xeric conditions below. Dozens of Sonoran scrub oaks welcome you into the oasis-like domain. These small trees sport spiky-toothed, leathery evergreen leaves and twiggy gray-brown branches coated in woolly fibers. Mule deer browse on their leaves, while many birds and rodents indulge in the plant's early fall acorn crop.

As you get closer to the rock wall up ahead, a wide range of plants fills in the gaps. Narrowleaf yucca—a perennial shrub with long, curly white fibers growing from tall, erect swordlike green leaves—can grow up to 7 feet tall. Meanwhile, keep an eye out for dwarf lupine, an annual wildflower with little blue-and-white nectar-rich flowers that attract lots of bees while synthesizing airborne nitrogen into a chemical dispersed underground that helps other plants grow. Another unusual yet common plant here is Torrey's

▸ A common chuckwalla vogues for the camera before darting under a sandstone overhang near the Hanging Garden trail.

▸ A stream orchid pops out from the wet wall underlying the hanging garden of maidenhair ferns.

jointfir, which reproduces through the spread of spores in its cones rather than seed dispersal like most other plants. And if it has rained recently, look for the sunflowery blooms of Parish's goldeneye. Some of the other flora found here in this desert panoply include woolly locoweed, blackbrush, rubber rabbitbrush, white prairie clover, broom snakeweed, desert willow, desert dandelion, fragrant sumac, roundleaf buffaloberry, and desert wishbone-bush, to name a few.

The trail tops out along a big sandstone wall decorated with abundant southern maidenhair ferns. You've reached the hanging garden. Precipitation from rain and snow collects on top and filters down through the porous Navajo sandstone, which is anchored below by a much less permeable layer of Kayenta rock, forcing the drip-drip-drip

to move horizontally and outward, where it nourishes this abundant fern colony below and the other plants you have just walked through. These pretty little colonizing ferns are constantly shedding tiny water droplets but don't feel wet to the touch. If you get close enough for a whiff, you won't be sorry: cosmetics companies use and synthesize maidenhair fern oil for shampoos and other health and beauty products.

▲ A healthy colony of southern maidenhair ferns—the hanging plants of the Hanging Garden—fills in the gap where the Navajo sandstone meets the underlying Kayenta rock and water seeps out sideways accordingly.

Enjoy the oasis-like setting here in the maidenhair mists under the shade of the overhanging rock. When you've had your fill, turn around and retrace your steps for the .75-mile walk back to the trailhead and parking lot. The short hike to the Hanging Garden, a unique ecosystem within a unique ecosystem, is well worth the minimal effort it takes to get there.

GLEN CANYON NATIONAL RECREATION AREA

BEEHIVE TRAIL AND THE NEW WAVE

Climb around on mesmerizing sand dunes frozen in time as rock and the eroded hoodoos surrounding them

	DIFFICULTY Moderate
LOCATION Southern Glen Canyon	LENGTH 1.4 miles
WHEELCHAIR ACCESSIBLE No	PETS ALLOWED Yes

We've all seen pictures of orange and white undulating sandstone waves in the Southwest—now's your chance to see them in person. Located just outside of Page, Arizona, and across the Colorado River in the Glen Canyon National Recreation Area, the New Wave and an adjacent formation nicknamed the Beehives were formed by wind and shifting sand dunes during the dinosaur days of the Jurassic period some 190 million years ago. These ancient dunes solidified over eons by means of a process called lithification, and these days have become quite a draw for visitors to the Southwest.

To get there, from Page's city center, drive north on S. Lake Powell Boulevard and then continue north on US-89, crossing the river on a bridge right next to the Glen Canyon Dam. Turn left onto Glen Canyon Dam Access Road, a sandy dirt road that's flat enough for regular cars to traverse, and then take the next right. Keep driving past the

The New Wave formed as successive compressed layers of sediment met the erosional forces of nature over almost 200 million years.

Beehives Campground to the designated parking area for Beehives area hikes. Put on your sunscreen, grab a full water bottle, and set out heading south on foot into the sandstone world of the Beehives.

The "trail" up over slickrock Navajo sandstone slabs can be a little challenging to follow, but the Beehives is a small formation and you would have a hard time actually getting lost. Keep moving southwest and feel free to wander in and out of the rock formations all around you. Named for their likeness to actual beehives, albeit much bigger, the Beehives here rise as high as 30 feet in some spots and feature grooved lines going in different directions. These desert oddities formed over eons via a geological process called cross-bedding, whereby different layers of silt are deposited on top of each other, each one affected by prevailing erosional forces (wind or water) at the time of its inception. Over millions of years, softer rock around the Beehives eroded away, leaving behind the otherworldly landscape we get to enjoy today.

While the hot sandy desert isn't known for plant life, certain species of flora nevertheless prevail. In late spring, starvation prickly pear cacti flower out in hot pink blooms with generous nectar supplies beloved by local bees and other flying insects. Like elsewhere across the desert Southwest, big sagebrush is common, perfuming the air as wind gusts pass. Notch-leaf scorpionweed plants send up erect, stalky rough green shoots topped off with little dark lavender flowers. Green ephedra, wax currant, alkali jimmyweed, and narrowleaf yucca colonize occasional free patches of sand between sandstone slabs. Bigger cracks in the rock provide opportunities for Utah juniper trees to take root.

As for wildlife, desert spiny lizards and chuckwallas dart underneath boulders, changing their appearance to blend in. Hawks, falcons, and golden eagles soar above in search of desert cottontail rabbits, ground squirrels, pocket mice, and kangaroo rats, while ravens scavenge everything from berries to other animals' kills to human trash. And as always when walking in the desert, watch where you step: you wouldn't want to surprise a rattlesnake looking for some peace and quiet underneath the low shade of some sagebrush.

Clockwise, from top left: A starvation prickly pear cactus blooms in hot pink under the Beehives.

Notch-leaf scorpionweed is one of the drought-tolerant species of flowering plants that thrives in the xeric setting of Southwest canyon country.

A Utah juniper is able to eke out an existence in the desert by sending a taproot as far as 15 feet below the surface (and lateral roots as much as 100 feet from the tree) to collect moisture and nutrients.

Keep walking by, through, and among the Beehives and after about a half mile of hiking, round the southern end of the formation and follow the trail as it curves around to the north. In another 0.3 mile or so, look for an indent in the layered sandstone above you and make your way up there by hook or by crook. There's no way to see the true glory of the New Wave without climbing up and over some sandstone fins, so make sure you are wearing good sneakers or hiking shoes and take it slow over this most uneven terrain. As you climb up into the natural bowl above you, you'll feel like you are being swallowed up by a wave of rock as undulating orange and white sandstone layers spread out all around you.

Not to be confused with the Wave—a similar, more famous wave-like sandstone formation some 40 miles to the west and only accessible to a limited number of visitors each day, who must compete in a daily lottery for the privilege of making the 6.5-mile hike across unmarked terrain—anyone can drive right up and check out the New Wave. Both the New Wave and the Wave formed when large wind-whipped sand dunes spread out across the region during the age of the dinosaurs. These dunes overlapped with one another and over time became compressed and cemented together in laminated striations, with differing resistance to erosion in each layer, depending on the constitution of the sediments present. Occasional rains would send water through these nascent layers of sandstone, following the path of least resistance, further widening any channels already present. Then the wind would take over, whipping through the gaps and depressions, carrying away minute particles of sand, further exaggerating the erosion process by sculpting deep troughs into the layer cake of ancient compressed sediments. Most of the sculpting happened eons ago, but erosion from wind, water, and, of course nowadays, human trampling means the process is ongoing—so see it while you can.

Spend as much time as you like enjoying the unearthly setting, and then make your way out of the bowl and back down to the flats around the formation. Keep heading north, walking along the west side of the formation (along the edge of the sandy road) for another 0.3 mile, go right at the intersection, and soon you'll see the parking area up ahead. You won't soon forget the natural beauty you encountered at the New Wave and the Beehives.

NAVAJO SLOT CANYONS

Follow a Navajo guide into a narrow red rock slot canyon and experience a whole new kind of sensory deprivation

DIFFICULTY
Easy

LOCATION
Navajo Nation, southeast of Page, Arizona

LENGTH
0.5 mile

WHEELCHAIR-ACCESSIBLE
No

PETS ALLOWED
No

If you're traveling through the Glen Canyon National Recreation Area and the city of Page in northern Arizona, then you are quite close to one or more of the region's famous slot canyons. The most astounding and easily accessed of these wonders of nature are located on the outskirts of Page, which happens to be the northwest corner of the 27,000-square-mile Navajo Nation, the largest Indian reservation in the United States. As such, you'll need to pay a Navajo guide to take you through any of the area's slot canyons, but being able to access these otherworldly sites is well worth the price of admission and the Navajo guides are founts of information about the region's human and natural history.

Whichever of the local slot canyons you visit—Lower Antelope, Upper Antelope, Antelope X, Secret, Waterhole, Mystical, Rattlesnake, Cardiac, or Cathedral—you won't be sorry. They all share the same dark and mysterious atmosphere, not to mention salmon-pink Navajo sandstone walls sculpted by the elements over eons into smooth and rounded textures.

▸ Some of the best views of Antelope Canyon X come from looking up.

Since all the slot canyons in the Page area are on Navajo land, expect to pay upwards of $50 per person to access any one of them with a Navajo guide leading the way. While each of the slots has its pros and cons, all of them deliver an amazing immersion into this sandy vertical red rock world.

Most visitors choose to tour either Upper or Lower Antelope Canyon, where millions of tourists before them have gotten great Instagram snaps of the sculpted orange-pink walls bisected by shafts of light. While it's well worth doing one or both of these tours if you've never seen a slot canyon, other choices will afford you a little more time and space. Also keep in mind that if you want to take photographs using a monopod or tripod, you'll have to find a specific "photographer's tour" (only offered in a few of the canyons, not including Upper and Lower Antelope)—but these are often the best ones to go on even for nonphotographers as they are less crowded and allow more free time to wander in and around whichever canyon you visit.

An excellent choice in this regard is the photographer's tour of Antelope Canyon X, which features smaller numbers but still packs a punch in terms of scenery. Book your preferred tour ahead of time online and when the time comes, head south on Coppermine Road and then east on Arizona State Route 98 (AZ-98) for 2 miles to the Taadidiin Tours parking area on the south side of the road. Show up fifteen minutes early to wait for your turn to board Taadidiin's four-wheel-drive truck for the bumpy 3-mile desert ride to the mouth of Antelope Canyon X.

After you get off the truck, follow your guide down into the gully ahead of you, which leads down about 300 feet between two sandstone hillsides to the entrance of the slot canyon. The profusion of plant life here is a welcome sight. During the American Southwest's July through September monsoon season, heavy rains pummel the desert and are funneled via the topography into this canyon, thus explaining why the hillside leading down into it has so much relative floral diversity.

To wit, keep an eye out for desert globemallow's spry minty green leaves that dress up nicely in spring with orange flowers centered on a yellow stigma. The upright

green sticks of Torrey's jointfir have an almost bamboo-like appearance and fill in a lot of the gaps in the sandy chute down into the canyon. Blue gama, a stalky grass that thrives in such xeric conditions, makes the most of this oasis-esque hillside. Rubber rabbitbrush, one of the most common plants of canyon country, dots the landscape, looking like a light green head of hair. Flatspine bur ragweed seems to train itself to follow the gaps between rock and sandy soil. Big bushes (5 to 8 feet wide) of Apache plume, with fluffy white tips of hundreds of tiny flowers, dominate cleavages between big slabs of sandstone where they can have some space to grow. Canaigre dock stands like a sentry as its big leathery, curvy leaves seem to compete with each other for sunlight. Panamint cryptantha, with its floppy little green shoots and fluffy white tips, and notch-leaf scorpionweed, with lettuce-like leaves and cute purple springtime flowers, make occasional cameos here as well. And if it's windy, chances are you'll see a tumbleweed or two blow by as a reminder you are in "roadrunner" country.

Keep walking down this geological funnel, which ancestors of today's Navajos used to herd desert bighorn sheep down to the western shore of the Colorado River. While you likely won't see any bighorns here these days—their population across Navajo country is down to about 5 percent of

Far left: Desert globemallow is one of many plants gracing this relatively lush stretch of desert.

Left: The sandstone walls get taller as the path leads down to the entrance to Antelope Canyon X.

Above: A common sagebrush lizard blends into its surroundings.

what it was before white settlement—keep an eye out for reptiles such as the common sagebrush lizard. These little guys measure between 2 and 3.5 inches long and feature gray, brown, and olive scales with hints of blue or green on their undersides; look carefully, as they blend in with the rocks they are sunning themselves on. Unlike warm-blooded endotherms (mammals and birds), which maintain functional body temperatures via an internal furnace of sorts, reptiles are ectothermic, or cold-blooded, meaning they rely on external temperatures to stay within a healthy and comfortable body temperature range—thus sunning themselves on a cool day to warm up or seeking cool shade on a hot summer day to cool down. These little sagebrush lizards subsist on a diet of ants, beetles, flies, and spiders, and are constantly looking over their proverbial shoulders for their chief predators around these parts: bullsnakes and birds of prey.

As you bottom out near the entrance to Antelope Canyon X, you'll notice a few sections of sandstone near the base of the cliffs that are pockmarked with holes. These are the makeshift residences of Ord's kangaroo rats, industrious local rodents that develop complex burrow systems with separate chambers for nesting, child-rearing, food storage, and sleeping. They also use the burrows for keeping cool

◂ Desert wire-lettuce and desert wishbone-bush are among the hardy plants eking out a living near the entrance to the slot canyons in the region.

and staying in the shade during the heat of the desert day. By night, these herbivores are out foraging for Indian rice-grass seeds, their primary food source, which they carry back home in their cheek pouches. Desert biology nerds laugh about their forgetfulness, as these rats sometimes husk and cache seeds and then abandon them in big piles for no apparent reason. They are also famous for their ability to change direction in midair when they jump, using their tails for balance.

Now that you are at the bottom, follow your guide to the right into the dark recess that is the beginning of Antelope Canyon X itself. It feels like you are sneaking through a secret door as you round the sculpted red rock sandstone corner and enter the dark and mystical domain within the slot canyon. The same salmon-pink sand that was everywhere outside this catacomb is now only there as a narrow "trail" at your feet between towering smooth sandstone walls. Looking up, you'll notice the rock slabs get pinker and lighter as you crane your neck to look for the sky. In fact, that sandstone is all the same color, but the gradations of light from the sun's rays make it look like different hues. At the top, some 125 feet above you, the canyon walls form around an X-shaped opening, giving this ancient canyon its modern nickname of Antelope Canyon X.

Make your way along this otherworldly pathway, sometimes squeezing between near pinch points in the canyon walls to get through. Around every twist and turn you can experience new views as the eroded walls curve in unique ways.

Just how do these slot canyons form? For starters, the Navajo sandstone that makes up the canyon walls—and all the rocks and boulders here as far as the eye can see—is geologically homogeneous, meaning it has a uniform mixture of minerals and grain size throughout. The upshot of the rock having this type of geological constitution is that it erodes uniformly, so water and wind can cut deeply into it and keep going down easily via the steep gradients that become the canyon sidewalls. The finishing touch on sculpting these slot canyon walls is the preponderance of heavy rain downpours during the monsoon season, when torrents of water funnel through, carrying rocks and sand and anything else in the way along for a wild ride. Indeed, you wouldn't want to be in here during a monsoon, as slot canyons like this play host to what is in essence a narrow, confined tidal wave of water 12 feet high carrying sticks and rocks. (If there are thunderstorms in the forecast the tours don't run.)

It's hard to believe that the erosional forces that formed these beautiful canyons began some 200 million years ago, when dinosaurs roamed the planet, and maybe even harder to believe that these seemingly solid rock walls are still being shaped and sculpted today.

There isn't much living inside the walls of the canyon. Plants don't get enough light or soil to survive, and animals have no business inside the slot canyon either, although occasionally snakes and lizards fall over the walls up top and end up trapped deep inside the canyon. If you see one, give it plenty of space to get by if you can.

Explore the quarter-mile short canyon for about a half hour and follow your guide back out when the time comes. Then explore another canyon "next door," which is actually the southern end of Antelope Canyon itself. The short walk between the two slots features some more greenery and feels like an otherworldly breezeway. Enjoy more red rock splendor inside this second catacomb-like slot, then make your way out and return the way you came to the truck, now well-versed on the details of the otherworldly world of slot canyons.

Secret Canyon is another tour worth looking into, especially as it can be combined with a stop at a private viewing area of Horseshoe Bend, overlooking the region's famous oxbow bend in the Colorado River from a unique vantage point on a red rock sandstone ledge 1000 feet above. The 25-minute drive over sandy backroads on the

▲ The Horseshoe Bend Overlook on the outskirts of Page, Arizona, is an iconic view of the American Southwest.

◂ Secret Canyon is also well worth a visit, especially when paired with a stop at the Horseshoe Bend Overlook.

tour company's open-air four-wheel-drive truck is an adventure in and of itself, only to be topped by the quarter-mile "hike" through Secret Canyon, with the "trail" threading the needle between undulating waves and twisting corkscrews of sandstone. Secret Canyon's sidewalls tower as much as 120 feet higher than the path.

Whether you visit one of the slot canyons detailed above or any of the others around here, you'll be raving about the experience to any friends and loved ones not accompanying you. Walking through a slot canyon, you can't help but marvel at the variation of natural beauty—and how lucky we are to behold it.

GRAND CANYON NATIONAL PARK

BRIGHT ANGEL TRAIL TO 1.5-MILE RESTHOUSE

Descent from South Rim to historic resthouse showcases Grand Canyon ecology and vistas

DIFFICULTY
Moderate to difficult, with steep return

LOCATION
South Rim, Grand Canyon

LENGTH
3 miles

WHEELCHAIR ACCESSIBLE
No

PETS ALLOWED
No

Perhaps the most famous and oldest trail in the Grand Canyon, the Bright Angel Trail has been used by humans for thousands of years as the primary route from the top down to the canyon floor over 6 miles and with a vertical drop of 3000-plus feet. While some adventurous hikers complete the out-and-back 12-miler in a day, and others backpack in and camp at Havasupai Campground along the Colorado River, most of us prefer to bite off only a bit of this epic trail, turning around at the 1.5 Mile Resthouse. This 3-mile out-and-back hike delivers outstanding canyon views and a good understanding of the landscapes and ecology of the national park.

If you're not already staying nearby at the South Rim in one of the park lodges or campgrounds, look for parking near the trailhead (behind the Bright Angel Lodge cabins). If those spots are all full, drive to the Backcountry Information Center's lot D, where you can park, and then make the seven-minute paved walk over the railroad tracks, following

◂ A mule train descends the Bright Angel Trail near the South Rim.

the sidewalk past Maswik Lodge before crossing another set of rail tracks and looking for the trailhead on the right. Alternatively, you can park at the Grand Canyon Visitor Center and then catch the free park shuttle bus—take the Village (Blue) Route, which will let you off near the Bright Angel Trailhead.

Make your way out towards the rim behind Bright Angel Lodge and look for a sign marking the trailhead along the edge across from the rock corral mule pens just west of Kolb Studio. As soon as you take the plunge past the trailhead sign, you lose elevation right quick. The trail is uniformly 4 feet wide all the way down, and mostly constructed of sand-covered stone footings.

▲ A pinyon pine on the canyon's edge is lit up at sunset.

After just 0.2 mile of hiking, you'll cross through the first of two tunnels where trail makers used dynamite to reroute the trail through a rock wall back in 1906. Holes in the rock on the left remain as permanent scars from the blasting. Just beyond this first tunnel, some ancient petroglyphs adorn an overhanging cliff along the uphill side of the trail. Another similar tunnel comes up at 0.75 mile from the trailhead, followed by a series of switchbacks traversing a steep section of cliff that seems endless. Don't forget to look up every now and again and drink in the otherworldly side canyon scenery.

Unlike the more exposed South Kaibab Trail that follows a ridgeline, the Bright Angel Trail follows a now-dormant fault line, winding its way down the back of a side canyon. As such, massive cliffs frame the views (and provide ample shade) along the first 4 miles or so of the trail. Ample seeps and springs along the sidewalls give the upper section of the trail an almost oasis-like feel.

Pinyon pine trees with crooked trunks and furrowed dark bark pop out of unlikely crevices where you would least expect a 25- to 40-foot-tall tree to grow. One of the most common trees along the South Rim, these small but mighty pines produce compact cones with large seeds—pinyon pine nuts—every year in fall. While these fatty and nutritious nuts make for a tasty treat for a wide range of birds and mammals, none love them as much as the pinyon jay, whose fate is intertwined with that of the tree.

This approximately 10-inch-long dusky blue-gray bird depends on pinyon nuts for sustenance, eating some on the spot as scavenged but storing thousands more in below-ground caches that they save to retrieve when other food is scarce. Some of these caches are forgotten or otherwise abandoned and sprout into the next generation of pinyon pines the following spring—so the tree is dependent on the bird as well.

As of this writing, the U.S. Fish & Wildlife Service is investigating whether or not the pinyon jay—whose population numbers are down by more than 85 percent over the last half-century as a result of the loss of pinyon-juniper habitat across the Southwest—should be added to the nation's list of endangered species. If and when the federal government lists the pinyon jay as threatened or endangered, it will mean much stricter laws and more stringent environmental reviews of potential development sites across the region so as to protect this habitat.

Another tree that grows near the rim and is beloved by wildlife is the Gambel oak. These 15-foot-tall deciduous trees with big floppy, leathery leaves produce acorns in fall that acorn woodpeckers go gaga for, hoarding and then caching them in holes they drill into dead tree snags called "granary" trees. One granary tree may have upwards of 50,000 holes in it, each of which is filled with an acorn. One or more of the birds is always keeping a lookout on the granary tree to ward off interlopers.

The crooked, twisted trunks of Utah junipers are also a common sight heading down toward 1.5-Mile Resthouse. A wide range of birds as well as coyotes eat the juniper berries and deposit the encased seeds in their droppings, helping propagate the plant far and wide.

Keep an eye out for prickly pear cacti, which flower out in yellow and other colors in late spring and summer. Oval red fleshy fruits called tunas ripen below the cacti's flowers and are enjoyed as a delicacy by a wide range

▾ Pinyon jays are on the ropes across their native territory due to the loss of their primary habitat to human development, wildfires, and insect infestations. And these threats are only exacerbated by global warming.

▲ The 1.5-Mile Resthouse was built by the Civilian Conservation Corps, a federally funded program to employ people to build out public infrastructure during the throes of the Great Depression.

of wildlife including antelope ground squirrels and coyotes.

An array of wildflowers adds pops of color throughout the midcanyon landscape. Deer goldenbush blooms out in sunflowery glory along the rock wall above the Bright Angel Trail. Navajo fleabane, an aster relative, features lavender-white petals surrounded by mustard-yellow centers, beckoning pollinators. Smallflower globemallow has fan-shaped coarsely toothed leaves and orange five-petaled flowers climbing up a central stalk during summer. And hoary tansyaster blooms in late summer with brilliant blue-purple petals surrounding a lemon-yellow stigma. Some other low-lying plants filling in here and there include Indian ricegrass, Fremont barberry, cliff fendlerbush, banana yucca, narrowleaf yucca, California brickellbush, rubber rabbitbrush, snakeweed, squirreltail, white sagebrush, green ephedra, fernbush, muttongrass, Utah agave, winterfat, dropseed, needlegrass, and miner's lettuce.

Keep moving down canyon and eventually you'll see a sign for the 1.5 Mile Resthouse and rock stairs heading up and to the right. Climb the twenty or so stairs to check out the resthouse, a primitive gable-roofed rock-and-timber shelter constructed in the 1930s by the Civilian Conservation Corps and featuring an interpretive display and panoramic views of the canyon out three sides. Enjoy the scenic beauty and the company of other hikers giddy to be in such a magical spot.

When you've enjoyed the canyon and camaraderie to your heart's content, refill your water bottle and use the vault toilet if needed—and steel yourself for the climb back out of the canyon, where you'll regain the 1120 feet in elevation you lost on the way down. Like anything great in life, you have to work for it. So put one foot in front of the other and soon you'll be back up at the South Rim, hopefully with some good pictures and definitely with some new memories to last a lifetime.

GRAND CANYON NATIONAL PARK

SOUTH KAIBAB TRAIL TO OOH AAH POINT

Close encounters with canyon walls and unique panoramas on rapid descent into the Grand Canyon

DIFFICULTY
Moderate

LOCATION
South Rim, Grand Canyon

LENGTH
1.8 miles

WHEELCHAIR ACCESSIBLE
No

PETS ALLOWED
No

Hiking from the South Rim down the South Kaibab Trail into the depths of the Grand Canyon itself is a rite of passage for anyone visiting America's most famous chasm. The short, fast, and most easily accessed way down offers not only an immersion into the details of the canyon walls but also panoramic views you won't get from anywhere else in the national park.

Get yourself to the well-marked South Kaibab Trailhead off the Yaki Point Road on the free shuttle—either the Kaibab Rim (Orange) Route or the Hiker's Express—or park at the lot just east of Yaki Point Road and walk back. If you are hiking here in the morning, you'll benefit from lots of shade as the sun isn't high enough in the sky yet to shine down over the canyon walls that the trail hugs. Otherwise, prepare for lots of sun exposure and no fresh water along the way.

Join the trail, constructed primarily of stone footings that are covered in thick deposits of sand, as it heads quickly down via a series of severe switchbacks, dropping some 200 feet in elevation within the first quarter mile of hiking before leveling out a little at a shallower decline for the rest of the mile down to Ooh Aah Point. Stop along this shallower gradient at will to take in (and photograph) the mid-canyon panoramas, including the seldom seen east walls of the Grand Canyon.

Given the steepness of the trail, there is hardly a profusion of plant life here. But the occasional seeps and springs in the canyon walls provide enough dripping moisture to support relatively healthy populations of plants. Pinyon pines and Utah junipers are among the trees that branch out from the occasional spots where they can put some deep roots down, while big sagebrush, snakeweed, dropseed, green ephedra, banana yucca, narrowleaf yucca, winterfat, Indian ricegrass, Utah agave, and needlegrass opportunistically fill in the gaps.

◂ Hikers descend on the South Kaibab Trail.

Likewise, don't expect to see a lot of wildlife on the way down to Ooh Aah Point—but be sure to keep your senses alert in case you do get to see something special. After all, the Grand Canyon is one of the few spots left in the world where you stand a chance to see wild California condors fly. These majestic and unmistakable scavengers, with their bald red heads, black bodies with triangular white patches under the wings, and wingspans topping 10 feet, soar on thermals above the canyon.

Indeed, condors, whose primary source of nutrition are the decaying remains of other dead animals, used to be common across what's now the Lower 48 until about 10,000 years ago when their numbers dropped precipitously. Not coincidentally, the condors' rapid decline in the fossil record syncs up with the timing of the mastodons and saber-toothed cats going extinct, presumably at the hands of humans who had crossed into the so-called "new world" via the Bering land bridge a few thousand years earlier. With no carrion to feed on, those primeval condors had nothing to eat and as such went extinct except for some small colonies up and down the West Coast. And many of the surviving birds succumbed to lead poisoning after scavenging on carcasses shot by hunters with lead ammo.

The federal government declared the species endangered in 1967, and by the early 1980s only 22 condors remained in the wild. In the early 1990s, biologists from the U.S. Fish & Wildlife Service captured and placed these remaining condors into a captive breeding program for four years before reintroducing them—along with some of their offspring—back into the wild at five locations around the West, including a dozen at Vermillion Cliffs, some 40 miles northwest of the Grand Canyon. These days upwards of 111 of the birds soar through the skies of canyon country, all descended from those original twelve. The Grand Canyon is, of course, one of the birds' favorite haunts in the region given their predilection for perching on high cliffs and sailing across the sky on thermals—not to mention the plethora of carrion

A dozen California condors were reintroduced into Southwest canyon country in the late 1990s; this initial population has multiplied ninefold in the intervening years, with many of the majestic scavengers calling the Grand Canyon and surroundings home.

▲ You can't beat the views of the Grand Canyon from the South Rim.

available on the canyon floor and on top of the rim for their dining pleasure.

Keep an eye out for condors, but another animal species you should definitely be aware of along the South Kaibab Trail are pack mules, which could be moving up or down canyon with a tour and a guide. If you see mules coming your way, yield to them and move to the uphill side of the trail, away from the edge. Listen for instructions from the mules' guide, and then resume hiking once the ungulate hybrids have moved 50 feet past you.

You should pay the same respect to (human) hikers coming out of the canyon as you are heading down. Yield to them as well and let them pass. You'll appreciate the same courtesy when you're hiking back up.

The National Park Service constructed this trail in the 1920s partly to circumvent profiteering commercial operators who built and charged for access to the Bright Angel Trail, which at the time was the only hiking trail down into the canyon. Meanwhile, the National Park Service built the North Kaibab Trail on the other side of the river, giving hikers the first rim-to-rim option.

Keep on hiking and about half mile in, you'll get to Yaki Point, a good spot for a swig of water and a photo of O'Neill Butte ahead of you with Skeleton Point in the distance. In just under another half mile, you'll arrive at Ooh Aah Point—you'll know you're there when you see the quaint wooden sign marking the spot. Revel in this unique perspective that most visitors to Grand Canyon National Park never get. There's never been a better time to get the panorama mode going on your smartphone.

Eat a snack and drink some water, because you've got a long climb back up if you are turning around here like most hikers on the South Kaibab Trail. You'll have to retrace your steps, but this time it will be gaining 600-plus vertical feet in under a mile. The distance may not be great—the total out-and-back hike clocks in at just under 2 miles—but it's still a calf burner. On the bright side, you'll get a better view of the plants on the way up given that you'll be focused more on putting one foot in front of the other than on the distracting glorious views that you saw on the way down. (More ambitious hikers who get an early start and carry plenty of

◂ The view from Yaki Point in the morning showcases the many layers of the Grand Canyon.

▴ Ooh Aah Point is an aptly named spot.

water can make a long day of it and continue on down canyon to dip their feet into the Colorado River at the bottom, some 5.5 hiking miles—and a mile in elevation!—below.) While you might be swearing on the way back up from Ooh Aah Point, as those switchbacks seem like they'll never end, you won't soon forget the experience of traversing inside the steep Coconino sandstone walls of the Grand Canyon.

GRAND CANYON NATIONAL PARK

SHOSHONE POINT

Trek through ponderosa pines to a dramatic, off-the-beaten path Grand Canyon overlook

DIFFICULTY
Easy

LOCATION
South Rim, Grand Canyon

LENGTH
2.1 miles

WHEELCHAIR ACCESSIBLE
No

PETS ALLOWED
No

The short 2.1-mile out-and-back hike to Shoshone Point gets you into northern Arizona forest primeval, away from the crowds and out onto one of the most thrilling overlooks in Grand Canyon National Park.

To get there, drive east from the Grand Canyon Visitor Center along the South Rim's Desert View Drive (Arizona State Route 64) for 3 miles and look for the unmarked parking area to the north, just west of mile marker 246. There is room for about sixteen cars but most likely only a few will be there as the throngs of tourists are all crowded by the South Rim, where most of the park's lodging and visitor amenities are located. Set out on foot past the gate, which blocks cars from following the double-wide, mile-long pathway you are following out to Shoshone Point.

◂ Hikers enjoying the view from Shoshone Point are dwarfed by the obelisk-like natural structure of Mushroom Rock.

▾ Ponderosa pines are the dominant tree in the forests surrounding the rim of the Grand Canyon.

Within a few steps you'll forget about the crowds as you become immersed in this classic northern Arizona forest. Ponderosa pine trees dominate here—stick your nose into the tree's bark and you can smell the sweet sap, which reminds some of vanilla. These trees are true survivors, living through freezing winters—5 feet of snow on the ground is typical for these parts by January every year—and sweltering summers with temps topping 100°F for days or weeks on end. Adding insult to injury are monsoon-like thunderstorms that pass through between July and September, sending flash floods into the forest and igniting wildfires with lightning strikes. Indeed, many of the bigger, older ponderosas here sport charred, black fire-scarred spots on their lower-trunks. Despite these harsh conditions, many of these trees live beyond their 500th birthdays.

Part of the reason they live so long is their natural resilience and a long coexistence with wildfire. Mature ponderosas have large plates of thick, reddish-orange bark that flakes off when it encounters flames. They also have deeper roots than other conifers, which helps them survive surface fires. Meanwhile, their long, waxy needles have a high moisture content, while their buds have thick scales that shield them from the extreme heat of surrounding flames, and the tree's typically open crown helps heat dissipate.

Historically, this region was beset with wildfires once every five to 25 years. This frequency of fires served to burn off low-lying grasses, shrubs, and small trees, maintaining a more parklike, open-stand setting for the remaining mature ponderosa pines. But decades of fire suppression in the region have led to the buildup of "fuel" —unburned tinder— on the forest floor, which has made wildfires more frequent and more intense in recent years. As a result, the National Park Service has begun a program of systematic prescribed burns in different parts of Grand Canyon National Park to burn off this tinder so actual wildfires are starved of the fuel they would need to spread widely.

While ponderosas may be king here, lots of other trees have a presence in the forest near the rim. Utah junipers twist and turn, growing from a single taproot that penetrates deeper than a typical tree's root system as an adaptation to the generally xeric environment and nutrient-poor soils hereabouts. This extracts water directly from underground water tables. Birds and coyotes help these trees propagate by feasting on their whitish-blue berries (seeds) and then depositing them elsewhere via their waste.

Another tree that fills in the midcanopy level is Gambel oak. In fall, these trees drop acorns, which are collected and cached by the local golden-mantled ground squirrel population. While the squirrels are pretty good at remembering where they leave their caches, some of the stockpiles are forgotten and sprout new sapling oaks the following spring, thus helping propagate this tree species in the region in general.

A wide range of shrubs and herbaceous plants fills in the gaps between trees here in this high-elevation forest. Desert phlox sprouts dozens of cute little five-petaled lavender flowers in spring. Thickleaf penstemon, a member

Clockwise, from above: Some of the spring and early summer wildflowers you'll see on the way to Shoshone Point include desert phlox, lobeleaf groundsel, thickleaf penstemon, and Indian paintbrush.

of the figwort family, grows stalky and straight and blooms in clusters of waxy violet basal leaves. Another common wildflower is the lupine, with narrow, elongated leaves growing in a ring at various points around the stem and bright, showy purple flowers in spring and early summer that point toward the sky. These humble yet beautiful little plants provide an important environmental service to the ecosystem by synthesizing airborne nitrogen into a chemical element that is used by other plants below the surface as fertilizer (in a process known as "nitrogen fixing"). They also attract bees, butterflies, and hummingbirds.

Lots of other wildlife pass this way as well. You may see a mule deer, named for its big ears, which resemble those of mules. These herbivores' diet includes grasses, flowering plants, shrubs, nuts, and berries. They avoid the heat of the day, especially in summer, by going about their daily activities at night and in the early morning when it's cooler. Their

large, pointy ears help them radiate body heat away, which also helps keep them cool. Mule deer's primary predator in these parts is the mountain lion, but their skittish nature and excellent hearing and eyesight are usually enough to help them live another day.

▲ An ancient Rocky Mountain bristlecone pine guards the edge of the canyon near the Shoshone Point Trail.

▼ Williamson's sapsuckers have drilled small holes into the furrowed reddish bark of this old ponderosa pine tree in search of sustenance in the form of sap and the inner bark (phloem) as well as any insects that become trapped.

Rocky Mountain elk, introduced to the Southwest a century ago, and bighorn sheep, which are natives here, are also known to graze in this area. If you see bighorn lambs frolicking on the rocks leading out to Shoshone Point, consider yourself lucky and give them plenty of space.

Keep moving along the double-wide dirt road that serves as the trail to Shoshone Point as it cuts straight through the forest. While you may not see many birds, given how dense the forest is, you'll definitely hear some. Birders may recognize the intermittent chirps and songs of swamp sparrows, western tanagers, Grace's warblers, and violet-green swallows, among others. But one bird you'll certainly hear (if not see) is the common raven. This corvid is one of the smartest birds, and its scrappy mentality means it can survive in a range of habitats, much like its urban cousin the crow.

▸ Mushroom Rock seems to erode away more every year, so check it out while you can.

Within twenty minutes or so, depending on your hiking pace, you'll arrive at an opening where you'll see several picnic tables, a covered pavilion with more tables, and a small bathroom structure. Welcome to the Shoshone Point picnic area. Walk over to the edge and take in the view of the Grand Canyon before finding your way to the trail that leads to a promontory jutting out into the canyon itself. While the hike until this point has been flat and through the woods, now things get vertiginous as you carefully pick your way along the decidedly single-track sandy trail that winds past dwarfed and wind-twisted western junipers and spriggy wildflowers such as the scarlet-red Indian paintbrush and pretty yellow lobeleaf groundsel. Watch your step over rocks and roots as you proceed past a 10-foot-tall balanced rock monolith eroded into the shape of a mushroom. Utah junipers cling to the edges of the cliff, sending their twisty branches skyward. Within just 0.1 mile you are at the end of the line, standing atop a huge rock ledge with Grand Canyon walls surrounding you in three directions.

This is your Kodak (or selfie) moment if there ever was one, so make sure to snap a few pics. Hang out as long as you like—it can get windy, so come prepared with a jacket—and then carefully retrace your steps back to the picnic area and trailhead having checked off another quintessential Grand Canyon experience.

GRAND CANYON NATIONAL PARK

CAPE ROYAL TRAIL

Hike through diverse North Rim forest to a unique, immersive Grand Canyon viewpoint

LOCATION North Rim, Grand Canyon	DIFFICULTY Easy
	LENGTH 1 mile
WHEELCHAIR ACCESSIBLE No	PETS ALLOWED No

If you find yourself visiting the North Rim of the Grand Canyon, the Cape Royal Trail is a perfect way to get yourself out to the rim and see the nation's great chasm—and the Colorado River at the bottom—from an unusual perspective. Cape Royal itself sticks out from the rim and the hike traverses its length, getting you out to the most southerly viewpoint on the North Rim.

To get there from the Grand Canyon Lodge on the North Rim, drive north on Arizona State Route 67 (AZ-67, also called North Rim Parkway) for 3 miles to Cape Royal Road. Turn right (east) on Cape Royal Road and follow it for 20 miles to where it dead-ends at the Cape Royal parking lot and trailhead.

The parking lot has room for a couple dozen cars, but unlike at the South Rim, you won't have to jockey for a parking spot. The North Rim gets 1 million visitors a year, while the South Rim, which is much easier to access by car, gets 5 million! If you have visited the South Rim, you'll especially enjoy how uncrowded it feels up here on the north side.

The out-and-back hike traverses an easy and flat mile of walking anyone can do, but those with a fear of heights might not like how close you get to the edge at the end. The paved, rock-lined trail is wide and relatively flat (and wheelchair-accessible) but with a slight grade down toward the rim-side overlook.

The forest on both sides of the trail here is full of a wide diversity of native plants genetically predisposed to thrive in these high, dry conditions. Ponderosa pines, pinyon pines, Utah junipers, and big sagebrush are well represented trailside, growing right up to the edge of the chasm in some cases. Arizona cliffrose, an evergreen shrub with gray, ragged bark that often spreads out wider than it grows tall, sports abundant yellow-white flowers in spring. Meanwhile, wax currant and its close cousin gooseberry produce lots of fall berries beloved by local birds and small mammals. And the scarlet-red blooms of Indian paintbrush decorate the landscape here and there in spring and early summer.

◂ Life on the North Rim at Cape Royal suits pinyon pines just fine.

One of the prominent features you can see from Cape Royal Point is Wotans Throne.

◂ Ringtails hunt throughout the forest of the North Rim, but you probably won't see them unless you do a night hike.

While there are a lot of plants vying for space and light, ponderosa pines rule this roost, just like across the way on the South Rim. At least one endemic wildlife species, the Kaibab squirrel, is dependent on these big, sweet-smelling pines. The small (approximately 20-inch-long) rodents are a subspecies of the Abert's squirrel that thrives in much larger numbers on and near the South Rim, and they are one of the rarest mammals in the national park system. Kaibab squirrels have dark gray backs featuring a red-brown patch, white bellies, and long, fluffy white tails. And like their Abert's cousins, they have large ears topped with tassels of fur. These high energy rodents stay busy scampering around in the tree canopy, jumping from branch to branch in search of the ponderosa's pinecones, buds, and twigs, which are their primary food source. They also feed on tree sap and fungi. In fact, their love of fungi is an important element in the functioning of the ecosystem here. When they dig up and eat ectomycorrhizal mushrooms, they disperse spores, aiding in fungal reproduction. Meanwhile, ectomycorrhizal fungi help ponderosa pines by growing around the trees' roots, which helps maintain moisture in the otherwise arid high desert environment here.

As for other wildlife, mule deer, black bears, Rocky Mountain elk, porcupines, and several other species of rodents call this coniferous forest home, but bighorn sheep, mountain lions, coyotes, skunks, raccoons, bobcats, foxes, and ringtails all make cameos here from time to time. The latter species, the ringtail, is most closely related to raccoons. These cat-sized carnivores—Arizona's state mammal—look like small foxes with long raccoon-like tails. Their flattened bushy tails with alternating black and white rings are almost as long as their heads and bodies. During daylight hours, they sleep in their dens, typically only coming out at night to hunt for birds, reptiles, amphibians, insects, and (their favorite) rodents. In fact, ringtails earned the nickname "miner's cat" because they were used by early white settlers in the West to control rodent populations in frontier mines. They can excrete a musky smell at will as a defense mechanism to deter foxes, coyotes, bobcats, and any other threatening predators.

After just shy of a quarter mile of hiking, take the side trail to the left (east) that leads out to Angel's Window, the only easily accessed natural arch in the Grand Canyon. The short detour is well worth a few extra steps as it leads out over the top of the arch itself, where you can get great views down into the canyon looking east. Snap a few pics, return back to the main trail, and make your way the last 0.2 mile to a fork where it lollipops out in a loop around to the canyon edge. Go either way and in a few more steps a panoramic view of the Grand Canyon opens up before you. A fence with metal rails and posts keeps visitors on the right side of the cliff. Indeed, the sheer drop-off here is severe—and you are almost 1000 feet higher in elevation than at the South Rim.

The red ridges and cliffs below are dotted with green as seeps and springs provide enough irrigation for this panoply of xeric plants to hang on for dear life. Looking across to the striated canyon walls, you get a great sense of the different sediment layers that make up the walls of the Grand Canyon from this "meta" view up here.

Standing at the tip of Cape Royal surveying the majestic canyon below and all around, you feel like you're floating above it all. Indeed, at an elevation of some 7880 feet, you just might be.

When you've been mesmerized enough, turn around and retrace your steps back to the parking lot, getting a different perspective on the trees and squirrels and flowers along the way. Cape Royal is an elemental place, and we are all lucky to be able to get to visit it.

GRAND CANYON NATIONAL PARK

BRIGHT ANGEL POINT

Cross through ponderosa pine forest to a classic overlook of eroded, striped Grand Canyon walls

DIFFICULTY
Easy

LOCATION
North Rim, Grand Canyon

LENGTH
1 mile

WHEELCHAIR ACCESSIBLE
No

PETS ALLOWED
No

The hike to Bright Angel Point on the Grand Canyon's North Rim provides some serious bang for the buck; the out-and-back 1-miler winds along a North Rim ridge and ends up at a small aerie jutting out into and over the Grand Canyon. The views along the way, and especially at the terminus at Bright Angel Point itself, are truly epic—you'd be remiss coming all the way to the North Rim without checking it out.

To get there, follow the park road (Arizona State Route 67) from the northern park entrance all the way to its terminus at the Grand Canyon Lodge on the North Rim. Find a spot in the parking lot there and then make your way on foot behind the lodge's veranda and look for the well-marked trailhead. The trail itself is paved and mostly level throughout except for a few steep sections and some stone stairs here and there (so it's not wheelchair accessible). While anyone in decent shape can make it out and back without even breaking a sweat—the total hiking distance is only a mile—those with a fear of heights might want to think twice given the vertiginous drops along both sides of the majority of this trail. Plus, the elevation of 8148 feet may be higher than you're used to, so take it slow, stay hydrated, and be aware of the signs of altitude sickness. Also, don't venture out to Bright Angel Point if there are thunderstorms passing through the area. That said, this short hike is far from risky—the National Park Service maintains the trail and railings to make sure no unnecessary accidents happen. And the visual payoff is huge, so don't let all that talk of steepness and lightning danger scare you. It's rare that a short hike on a paved path could qualify as epic, but the hike to Bright Angel Point must be an exception.

Start out on the trail as it funnels you onto the crest of a ridgeline that zigs and zags its way southeast towards Bright Angel Point. One especially narrow section early on feels like a roller-coaster ride except that you are on foot.

◂ Each horizontal layer of rock in the walls and fins of the Grand Canyon represents millions of years of geological history.

▲ A hiker surveys the view from Bright Angel Point (elevation 8148 feet) on the North Rim of the Grand Canyon.

As you run this vertiginous gauntlet of a trail, lots and lots of flora keep you practically swaddled in green. Like all around the canyon rim, ponderosa pines are the dominant tree species. But out here there are just as many Utah junipers twisting their trunks every which way and pinyon pines growing into perfect (if a bit oversized) Christmas trees as there are ponderosas. Subalpine fir, desert mountain mahogany, white fir, and quaking aspen—all native to the area but more common in other lower elevation parts of the national park—make occasional appearances. Scraggly little New Mexico locust trees fill in some of the gaps between bigger trees along the cliffsides, while crucifixion thorn, chaparral (creosote), and ocotillo pop up here and there opportunistically.

Given the vertical setting here at Bright Angel Point, birds are the most common form of wildlife you'll see (or hear). Given its prime location sticking out into the canyon,

dozens of bird species use the trees and cliffs here to roost and nest, not to mention as jumping-off points for aerial hunting forays. Given that the park takes up some 1900 square miles and is surrounded by human development, it's no wonder that birds flock here. In fact, more than 370 different bird species call different sections of Grand Canyon National Park home, with some 80 additional species migrating through every year.

High up on the North Rim is a raptor's paradise. Indeed, the Grand Canyon is a major stopover for migrating raptors every fall. If you're here then, keep your eyes and ears peeled for northern harriers, broad-winged hawks, Swainson's hawks, red-tailed hawks, ferruginous hawks, northern rough-winged hawks, Cooper's hawks, sharp-shinned hawks, American kestrels, merlins, bald eagles, ospreys, and turkey vultures.

Of course, lots of other birds besides raptors are present here, whether or not you see them. White-throated swifts live in the cliffs of the canyon walls and primarily feed on airborne bugs they catch "on the wing." Ravens, evening grosbeaks, American goldfinches, Steller's jays, wild turkeys, and seven different species of hummingbirds are frequently spotted by visitors hereabouts as well. In fact, the Grand Canyon as a whole was designated a Globally Important Bird Area by the National Audubon Society in 2014 to recognize and celebrate the role the park plays in providing safe haven for hundreds of bird species in the increasingly developed and urbanized world surrounding it.

As you get closer to Bright Angel Point, you'll cross over a short footbridge constructed by the National Park Service so hikers can traverse a chasm between two big underlying boulders. Keep moving and soon enough views of the canyon will open up in front of you. Even if it's not your first time, seeing the Grand Canyon takes your breath away.

Looking out and across is like a visual geology lesson that takes you back some 1.8 million years when the lowest layers at the bottom of the Grand Canyon, known to geologists as the Vishnu group, were formed. Still toward the bottom of the canyon but slightly above Vishnu is a layer called Tapeats sandstone. Moving on up are Bright Angel shale, Muav limestone, Redwall limestone, Supai group (a mix of shales, limestones, and sandstones), Hermit shale,

A footbridge helps hikers cross between huge boulders near Bright Angel Point.

Coconino sandstone, Toroweap limestone, and Kaibab limestone, which only appears at the tips of some of the least eroded monolithic walls, towers, and fins. The baby of the group, Kaibab limestone, lithified from sediment into rock some 270 million years ago. (The canyon itself didn't start to form until 5 to 6 million years ago.)

Each layer has different coloration, with the oldest and lowest layers being darkest, while the midlayers tend to contain more iron ore and as such feature red coloration more prominently. Meanwhile, the upper layers trend toward a chalky white.

Looking down into Bright Angel Canyon, you can discern a fracture in the Earth's crust that led to a fault where the sedimentary rock layers on the left rise higher than those on the right. At the bottom, a full mile below where you're standing on Bright Angel Point, Bright Angel Creek follows the contours of the fault line and eventually empties downstream into the much larger Colorado River.

When you've gotten your fill of Bright Angel Point, retrace your steps back to the parking lot and be sure to stop off at the main building of the Grand Canyon Lodge to get a hot drink and check out the late 1920s-style rustic architecture that this and other structures at the Grand Canyon helped make famous. The fact that the hike to Bright Angel Point is so short frees you up for more North Rim exploration the same day. Whether you hit some longer hikes near the lodge or drive over to Cape Royal, you can't go wrong here at the beautiful and less crowded North Rim.

PETRIFIED FOREST NATIONAL PARK

PAINTED DESERT RIM TRAIL

Overview hike showcases petrified wood examples against a sublime backdrop of glowing red Painted Hills

DIFFICULTY
Easy

LOCATION
North-central Petrified Forest

LENGTH
1.2 miles

WHEELCHAIR ACCESSIBLE
No

PETS ALLOWED
No

While the Petrified Forest National Park in eastern Arizona has a lot of cool sights and invigorating hikes, the one thing to do if you are only passing through or have limited time to explore is hike the Painted Desert Rim Trail. This out-and-back 1.2-miler showcases the small national park's unique collection of desert flora as well as the famous painted hills, which glow red at sunrise and dusk.

To get there, follow Interstate 40 (US-40) east from Holbrook, Arizona, for 24 miles and take exit 311, then cross over the highway heading north on Park Road, which leads into the national park. From the Petrified Forest National Park entrance sign, drive another third of a mile to the park entrance station (where you can pay the entrance fee or show your annual parks pass) and visitor center, where you can stop in to get oriented if you want. Otherwise, keep driving north and in another 1.3 miles pull into the small parking lot on the right (east) for Tawa Point. Park the car and head out on foot, first checking out the view from the overlook at Tawa Point.

From this spot on the canyon rim, you can see for hundreds of miles on a clear day, but it's the view of the Painted Desert down below in front of you that's most captivating. Indeed, the vista of this eroded mesa is a perfect introduction to what makes this small park so special. Red-and-brown-striped badland hills, part of what geologists have dubbed the Chinle Formation, cluster in small groupings against the otherwise sagebrush green landscape. These reddish-tinged badlands are composed of layers of lithified (turned to rock) sediment and ash deposited over many millennia beginning in the Triassic Period some 250 million years ago. Back then, the desert we see here today was a lush, subtropical equatorial forest near the northwestern edge of the singular supercontinent Pangaea.

Tall trees swayed along fast-moving rivers. Broad ferns, lush cycads, and huge horsetails waved in the tropical breeze. Giant reptiles and amphibians as well as early dinosaurs roamed the terrestrial habitat while huge ray-finned fish, freshwater sharks, coelacanths, and lungfish dominated the waterways. We know this because the fossil record in the eroding badland hills and elsewhere in the region tells no lies about the profusion of plant and animal life present during those prehistoric old days (some 200-plus million years before humans emerged as a distinct species).

The fine-grained rock layers of these badlands formed sequentially as silt, sediment, and volcanic ash settled onto the ground, deposited either by inundation with water (flooding) or by the wind. Volcanic eruptions during the Triassic and subsequent periods blanketed the atmosphere with ash, which shows up in the layers as well. Varying amounts of iron and manganese give each of the sedimentary layers their own unique hue within the dark red to brown spectrum. Like elsewhere across canyon country, only because the top layers have eroded over millions of years can we even see these amazing landscape features today.

The panoramic view from Tawa Point out into the eroded Painted Desert mesa is indeed enchanting, but there is much else to see in this neck of the desert, so continue on along the trail as it zigzags west and then north along the edge of the canyon. The well-worn dirt-gravel trail is wide and mostly flat, although a bit too rough (and with occasional "waterbars" to ease foot travel during the muddy

▲ The red-and-white-striped badlands of the Painted Desert seem to glow in the late afternoon sun.

monsoon season) to be easy with strollers, or wheelchairs, for that matter.

While the colorful geology steals the show, nature lovers will also appreciate the plant life that thrives here despite the arid conditions. These xeric (dry-adapted) plants have evolved various adaptations in response to environmental stimuli over the millennia.

To wit, look for narrowleaf yucca, which has long, spiny leaves that channel any moisture in the air to the plant's center, while its long, thick roots seek out and store water underground. Crispleaf buckwheat grows low to the ground and/or in a ball shape to reduce exposure to wind and to conserve water. Green ephedra has wax on its stems and leaves, which helps to seal water inside, especially useful when hot, dry winds blow through. And desert globemallow, which blooms out in delicate orange flowers in spring, sports pale downy hairs on its leaves that reflect strong sunlight and deflect drying desert winds.

Meanwhile, Indian paintbrush sends up unmistakable scarlet-red blooms in spring and early summer that indeed look like you could do brushstrokes with them. These "hemi-parasitic" flowers may look pretty but they don't always play nice, sometimes latching onto other plants' roots to pirate resources such as water, nutrients, and minerals.

Not a lot of trees grow out here in the desert, but you will encounter some Utah junipers. These 10- to 20-foot-tall trees have twisty trunks and typically one taproot that can reach 25 feet below the surface in search of water and nutrients, as well as lateral roots that can extend for upwards of 100 feet from the trunk.

Another tree you'll see around here is the pinyon pine, which grows upwards of 10 feet tall and has an extensive root system that often mirrors the size of the aboveground tree. The tree's compact cones contain protein-rich seeds—a pound of them contains more than 3000 calories—which are beloved (and cached) by local white-tailed antelope squirrels.

Speaking of rodents, plants aren't the only living things that have adapted to the hardscrabble life here—lots of wildlife call the Painted Desert and environs home. The most visible are mule deer, but lucky visitors might also get to spot pronghorn, coyote, kit fox, bobcat, badger, striped skunk, black-tailed jackrabbit, desert cottontail, desert shrew, porcupine, or Gunnison's prairie dog, not to mention six species of bat and eighteen different rodent species.

Meanwhile, some 258 different bird species have been spotted in the national park. Year-round avian residents include common ravens, house finches, greater roadrunners, horned larks, and red-tailed hawks, among others. Dark-eyed juncos, mountain bluebirds, and white-crowned sparrows are some of the birds that overwinter here, while barn swallows, black-headed grosbeaks, burrowing owls, and lark sparrows are summer-only residents. And in both spring and fall, dozens of additional species of migratory birds pass this way, including rufous hummingbirds, cedar waxwings, hermit thrushes, mountain bluebirds, and ruby-crowned kinglets.

Reptiles also have a commanding presence here, with sixteen varieties calling the park home. Indeed, lizards and snakes play an important role in maintaining overall

Clockwise, from top left: Purple three-awn is one of dozens of species of wild grasses native to the deserts of the American Southwest.

Like elsewhere across canyon country, big sagebrush is one of the most common plants alongside the Painted Desert Rim Trail.

Utah junipers don't have a lot of competition out here, and as such grow not only tall but especially wide.

Beep beep! The roadrunner is a Painted Desert native.

ecosystem health by gobbling up large quantities of insects, spiders, and scorpions, as well as other reptiles and even small mammals, thereby helping to prevent infestations by a single "pest" species.

As ectotherms (cold-blooded animals), these reptiles regulate their body temperature via external sources, unlike us mammals who walk around with an internal furnace keeping things just right. Snakes and lizards thrive here because they don't have to use much energy staying warm, thanks to the Arizona sunshine, and can instead get down to business finding food and reproducing. Of course, sometimes even the desert can get cold, which is when lizards and snakes hibernate by slowing down their metabolisms and entering an inactive torpor.

Keep an eye out for plateau fence lizards, as these little 3-inchers with black chevron-shaped scales up their backs like to sun themselves on exposed rock faces. Long-nosed leopard lizards and New Mexico whiptails are also common hereabouts. As for snakes, watch where you step—you wouldn't want to roust a desert striped whipsnake,

Chihuahuan nightsnake, or, heaven forbid, a prairie rattlesnake. The latter will usually warn you if you are getting too close by shaking its buzzing rattles. The good news is that these rattlers aren't particularly interested in injecting their venom into you as humans are not their prey. But watch where you step because anything can happen when an animal is startled or feels trapped or cornered.

Some other reasons to watch where you step include tarantulas, harlequin bugs, sun spiders, and velvet ants. These are just a few of the creepy crawlies you may encounter here if you're (un)lucky. While their bites won't kill you, you're better off avoiding them if you can. Live and let live is always the best policy.

Another small life-form you wouldn't want to squish is a frog or salamander. Believe it or not, amphibians abound around here, although you may not see them unless it's late summer monsoon season. While they've been in this part of the world in one form or another since the Triassic Period 200-plus million years ago, the present-day amphibian lineup here includes the western tiger salamander, the Arizona tiger salamander, and six species of toad, three of which are "spadefoots," meaning they burrow underground using specialized "spades" on their hind feet. Once they dig in, these spadefoot toads spend most of their time underground in earth-filled burrows in order to stay cool and safe from predators, only coming out during monsoon season to mate. Amphibian populations are declining everywhere around the planet as a result of a host of factors, including habitat loss, water contamination, ozone layer depletion, and global warming, and protected lands like this one play an important role in providing at least some habitat for them to call home.

Indeed, the outstanding eroded mesa views to the east and enchanting desert environment to the west make for an enjoyable hike chock full of natural beauty. Keep moving and eventually the trail leads out to Kachina Point, 0.6 mile from where you started at Tawa Point. It feels like you are standing on the bow of a big ship as you peer out over the red badlands from Kachina Point.

When you've had your fill, check out the Painted Desert Inn building right nearby. This historic structure was built in the 1920s (originally out of petrified wood!) as a small

Above, from left: A few small shrubs manage to grow on the badlands themselves, but the constant erosion means they won't last long.

Yellow stalks of desert prince's plume add a little natural bling to the otherwise adobe-red and sage-green setting.

inn and rest stop along what used to be U.S. Route 66 (now US-40). Due to structural problems—it was built on bentonite clay, which expands significantly during rainy periods—the building was reconstructed with local ponderosa pine timbers and adobe walls in the 1930s. These days it serves as a small museum featuring murals by Hopi artist Fred Kabotie as well as displays highlighting the building's history, the Depression-era Civilian Conservation Corps that rebuilt it into its present day "parkitecture" style, and Old Route 66, which used to pass right nearby. If the museum is closed, do a loop around the exterior at least to admire the adobe architecture and how well it blends into the natural surroundings.

Getting back to your car at Tawa Point is as easy as retracing your steps along the Painted Desert Rim Trail, or you can walk along the road nearby if it's getting dark or you want a change of scene. Either way it will be a little over a half mile to get back, at which point you can hike south from Tawa Point on what's called the Tawa Trail for additional views out in the mesa, or drive on to your next destination. The natural beauty all around and the lack of crowds make this off-the-beaten-path trail (and park) well worth a visit for anyone touring around Four Corners canyon country.

PETRIFIED FOREST NATIONAL PARK

BLUE MESA TRAIL

An otherworldly landscape of blue, purple, and white rounded badlands beckons exploration

	DIFFICULTY **Easy**
LOCATION **South-central Petrified Forest**	LENGTH **1 mile**
WHEELCHAIR ACCESSIBLE **No**	PETS ALLOWED **Yes**

The Blue Mesa Trail curves through a 1-mile loop that takes visitors down into and through the middle of an eroded mesa full of blue, purple, and white rounded eroded bentonite badlands that feel right out of some long-lost Dr. Seuss story.

To get there from Holbrook, Arizona, head east on U.S. Route 180 (US-180) for 17.5 miles, then turn left (north) on Petrified Forest Road. Follow it north for 12.8 miles and then turn right (east) onto Blue Mesa Scenic Road, which leads you another 2.7 miles to a small parking area that holds a dozen or so cars. Be sure to pull over along the way to check out the Teepees, an interesting set of striped maroon, white, and slate-blue badlands, also part of the Chinle Formation, just over 2 miles north of the turnoff for Blue Mesa Scenic Road. Or, if you are coming from points east, take exit 311 off Interstate 40 (US-40) and head north on Park Road, which becomes Petrified Forest Road as it winds around to eventually head south for 15 miles before hooking a left onto Blue Mesa Scenic Road, which leads 2.7 miles to the parking lot. Begin the hike from the trailhead behind the sun shelter at the Blue Mesa overlook.

◂ When you see the Teepees off the Petrified Forest Road, you know you are getting close to the Blue Mesa Trailhead.

▸ Saltbush, desert globemallow, and bitterbrush (left to right) are just a few of the hardy xeric plants that thrive here despite the harsh conditions.

From the get-go, you'll start out traversing a knife-edge ridgeline with panoramic views on both sides. Statuesque eroded hoodoos stand like minarets along otherwise smoothly sloping hillsides. Broom snakeweed, narrowleaf yucca, big sagebrush, saltbush, western needlegrass, bitterbrush, and desert globemallow cling to the steep hillsides. Metal railings along a few sections might ease the worries of parents of small children, but nevertheless be careful. The trail surface is primarily asphalt (but parts of it are too steep for wheelchairs).

After 0.1 mile the trail starts heading down quickly, losing about 100 feet in elevation over the next 0.1 mile via a series of switchbacks. It doesn't seem too bad going down, but remember to save some energy for the end when you'll have to hoof it back up here. As you descend, you'll

Clockwise, from above: A chunk of orange petrified wood is surrounded by the otherworldly blue, white, and purple badlands of the Blue Mesa.

The asphalt path into the Blue Mesa may as well lead to another world.

This view down into the Blue Mesa from up top showcases the power of wind and water as erosional forces.

essentially be going back in time as you get a close-up view of different stratified layers in the eroded badland hills.

Once you're down to the bottom, the trail levels off and you can choose which way to go around the lollipop loop. Either way will take you on a rolling trek through the eroded Blue Mesa. The mounds in here are colored in different striations—lavender purple, slate blue, dusky peach, and chalk white—based on the mineral content of each successive sedimentary layer. These badlands are part of the same geological formation (the Chinle Formation) as their red cousins in the Painted Desert to the north, but the mineral content here is different enough to give these eroding hills their own cooler color palette.

Badlands form wherever poorly consolidated rock is subjected to sporadic but torrential rain. The soft rock funnels

This tree dates back more than 200 million years when it was buried in wet sediment and ash, eventually turning to stone before being unearthed due to the erosion of the Blue Mesa.

gushes of water down rills, gullies, and washes along with loads and loads of sediment. The sediment-laden water flows cut deeper and deeper channels into the soft rock. Over time, these channels can become canyons. The sediment builds up at the bottom of the canyon, where it is eventually buried, and over many millennia, becomes lithified (turned into rock).

One of the main components of these badlands is bentonite clay, which is derived from the weathered combination of sediments and volcanic ash. Part of the reason these badlands have eroded so substantially here is the fact that this form of clay swells up during rainy periods and then shrinks and cracks when it dries out, creating an "elephant skin" surface. Beneath that, an intricate maze of natural chutes and voids creates a form of natural plumbing that helps channel water down and away. Sinks and seeps show up as dimples on the surface of the ever-eroding badlands, unearthing where these natural voids formed below. Some of these dimples eventually turn into larger caves or even natural bridges.

Take your time winding your way around the lollipop loop and indulging in the experience of wandering through and between these otherworldly badlands. You may as well be on another planet.

Chunks of petrified wood lay unadulterated along the trailside here and there, seemingly glowing in the hot sun in crystallized ochres, yellows, and whites. These tree trunk sections were buried in wet sediments saturated with dissolved minerals back in the Triassic Period. The lack of oxygen slowed the wood's decay, allowing minerals to replace cell walls and crystallize in place. The only reason we can see these chunks nowadays is the erosion of the layers and layers of lithified sediment that had built up around them over eons.

Most of the petrified logs we see here look like a logger chainsawed one slice out of a tree trunk and left it alone on the ground. But in fact, these tree trunk pieces were part of larger fallen trees—knocked down by wind, lightning, or floodwaters. They are broken into parts because the minerals that have replaced their wood fiber are brittle, and crack easily—so pieces break off along stress points where a tree might be laying down along uneven terrain. Some of the

▲ A piece of petrified wood is shaped like a mushroom as the harder capstone has stayed in place while water has worn away the rest.

petrified wood chunks are shaped in the form of mushroom-like pedestals due to water erosion wearing away the softer rock and leaving the harder capstones in place, although they will eventually fall to the ground as well. These unusual shapes are just part of the picture that makes this hike feel like you're walking on some kind of weird moonscape.

When you're ready to return to Earth as we know it, hustle on around the loop and make your way back up the approach trail, which no doubt seems a lot more difficult than when you descended it a half hour or so ago. You can feel good about yourself when you get to the top and see other people just stopping at the overlook for the view without doing the hike itself. Indeed, the Blue Mesa Trail is one of the best ways to familiarize yourself with what makes the Petrified Forest National Park such a worthwhile place to visit.

CRYSTAL FOREST

Tour a fallen forest of crystalline multicolored pieces of petrified wood glistening in the desert sun

DIFFICULTY
Easy

LOCATION
Southern Petrified Forest

LENGTH
0.8 mile

WHEELCHAIR ACCESSIBLE
Yes, but some steep grades

PETS ALLOWED
No

Hiking the 0.8-mile Crystal Forest Trail is one of the best ways to get up close and personal with the namesake feature of Petrified Forest National Park. Indeed, chunks and trunks of crystalline petrified wood lay scattered all along the short and flat lollipop loop trail, glinting in the desert sun.

To get there from Holbrook, Arizona, head east on U.S. Route 180 (US-180) for 18 miles to the national park's south entrance, where you'll turn left (north) and follow Petrified Forest Road for 15 miles to the Crystal Forest turnout and parking area on the east side of the road. From the park's north entrance and points east, follow Petrified Forest Road for 19.5 miles as it heads north and then curves south to the Crystal Forest turnout.

The short spur trail from the parking area to the loop is lined on both sides with big sagebrush, desert needlegrass, and alkali sacaton, among other xeric plants. Sprigs of the latter plant, often growing alongside petrified logs, look a little like wheat stalks scattered throughout the landscape. Mule deer, jackrabbits, and birds love to forage on

Clockwise, from above: This detail of a petrified log shows the rich color patterns caused by the mineralization of the wood hundreds of millions of years ago.

A black blister beetle feeds on a specklepod milkvetch plant; these half-inch long insects deter would-be predators by emitting a body fluid that contains the natural toxin cantharidin—so keep your distance.

The starvation prickly pear cactus blooms out in yellow and sometimes red flowers every spring.

the plant's stalks and small seeds. Alkali sacaton grows so well naturally in tough conditions—like here in the Arizona desert—that it is often used to seed disturbed landscapes like oil well pits and saline waste from power plants. Dozens of other species of drought-tolerant native plants vie for space and light across the desert as far as the eye can see.

At the fork in the trail, go either way and wind your way around, stopping to look at the abundant examples of petrified wood that have been here for more than 200 million years. Every tenth of a mile or so around this short loop features different examples of these ancient logs. They look just like regular logs until you get up close and can see the crystallized bright colors where the wood grain used to be. Also, it looks like a logger chopped up various tree trunks into smaller sizes but in fact these logs broke apart naturally as the quartz and other minerals now constituting their "guts" easily crack along fault lines.

How did this wood become petrified and how has it been able to remain more or less intact here for so long? The petrifaction process began some 225 million years ago when the land you see before you was a subtropical forest near the west coast of Pangaea, the singular supercontinent that encompassed all the land on the planet during the Triassic Period. Storms, flooding, volcanic eruptions, and other natural events would knock over, displace, and sometimes move entire uprooted trees into new locations.

Depending on the timing, some of these trees would get quickly buried in sediment flows, which would prevent them from being eaten by organisms or from decomposing (since they were encased without oxygen). Once buried, the trees' wood fiber decayed as groundwater rich in silica and other minerals rushed in; this process is known as mineralization or silicification. The minerals crystallized within the cellular structure of the wood, preserving the logs' original shape and structure but giving them an entirely different color palette (and earning it the nickname "rainbow wood"). For example, silica, the most common mineral involved in the petrifaction process, tinted parts of the resulting petrified wood quartz an almost translucent white, while iron oxides

◂ Silica creates the white quartz while iron oxides are responsible for the ochres in this piece of ancient petrified wood.

▲ This intact ridgeline on the outskirts of the Crystal Forest shows just how much earth has eroded away over the last 200-plus million years to expose the petrified logs on display here.

imparted shades of red, yellow, purple, or brown. Over millions and millions of years, erosion has worn away the rock layers that had encased this so-called rainbow wood underground, exposing it so we can nowadays appreciate its colorful, glinting glory.

Most of the petrified wood samples left here for us to ogle are from a long extinct species of conifer that biologists have dubbed *Araucarioxylon arizonicum*. These ancient trees could grow up to 195 feet tall with trunk diameters topping 9 feet across. Based on fossil imprints, they are believed to have had slender branches widely spaced around the entire trunk that were bent upwards at approximately 30-degree angles, with thinner branches in small clusters near the tip. While *Araucarioxylon arizonicum* appears to have been dominant, at least eight other species of fossil trees—all long extinct—have been found around the national park.

You can hike the loop in 20 minutes if you're in a hurry to get on the road and see more elsewhere, but if you have time to linger it's fun to stare at the different crystal patterns in so many of the petrified logs at rest here. Mother Nature is indeed a great designer, and her work is on full display in this slice of the northern Arizona desert.

PETRIFIED FOREST NATIONAL PARK

GIANT LOGS TRAIL

Commune with huge trunks and chunks of petrified wood

DIFFICULTY
Easy

LOCATION
Southern Petrified Forest

LENGTH
0.7 mile

WHEELCHAIR ACCESSIBLE
Yes, but some stairs

PETS ALLOWED
Yes

If you've only visited the Painted Desert in the northern section of Petrified Forest National Park and were disappointed with how little petrified wood is actually there, don't miss the Giant Logs Trail down south. Here you'll find some of the largest, most colorful petrified logs as well as Old Faithful log, which is from the largest of all the Triassic Period petrified trees unearthed so far.

To get there from Holbrook, Arizona, head east on U.S. Route 180 (US-180) for 18 miles to the national park's south entrance, where you'll turn left (north) and follow Petrified Forest Road for 2 miles to the well-marked Giant Logs parking area and trailhead. From the park's north entrance and points east, follow Petrified Forest Road for 26 miles as it heads north and then curves south to the Giant Logs turnout.

Set out on foot and follow the footpath behind the Rainbow Forest Museum to pick up the Giant Logs Trail as it forks off to the right. The dirt-and-sand trail is lined with cement edging on each side to help reduce erosion and keep hikers on the straight and narrow so as to minimize disturbances to the petrified wood, plants, and cryptobiotic soil

Scattered and petrified remains of 215 million-year-old extinct conifer trees are all over the place alongside the Giant Logs Trail in Petrified Forest National Park. ▸

(the nutrient-rich dark brown soil crust that helps build up the underlying dirt for other plants) of this highly visited part of the national park. Within a few steps you are immersed in the Rainbow Forest itself, with brown, gray, and quartz-white logs and stumps of 215 million-year-old trees scattered all over the desert floor on each side of the trail.

Some 225 million years ago, the lush subtropical forest here was home to towering *Araucarioxylon arizonicum* trees, which are distant ancestors to today's monkey puzzle trees. Over time, some trees died naturally or succumbed to storms, falling into rivers that snaked through the landscape. These giants began a journey downstream, eventually forming logjams. Volcanic eruptions blanketed the region with ash, burying the submerged logs under layers of sediment, which sealed them off from oxygen, preventing decay. Mineral-rich water, especially silica from volcanic ash, seeped into the buried logs. Over millions of years, this silica slowly replaced the organic wood, molecule by molecule, essentially turning them into stone. Millions of years of erosion gradually stripped away the layers of rock and sediment, revealing the petrified logs we see today.

A starvation prickly pear cactus fits right in alongside the other xeric plants that seem to thrive here despite living in what some would consider to be a desert wasteland.

▲ Pronghorn, desert bighorn sheep, and mule deer are among the wildlife species that consider the fruits of the cane cholla a tasty snack.

A spur trail leads to a plaque on a boulder celebrating Stephen Mather, the first director of the National Park

Clockwise, from top left: Lichens, one of the most widespread of all organisms on the planet, colonize petrified wood where they can.

Some of the largest petrified logs in the world are here in the Rainbow Forest along the Giant Logs Trail.

A desert globemallow plant growing alongside a chunk of petrified wood provides a pop of color with its orange late spring bloom.

Service. The little rise of land where the plaque is also plays host to several more pieces of petrified wood.

Back on the main trail, continue hiking up a small incline with large, rounded boulders off to your right and a profusion of plant life all around. Desert needlegrass, narrowleaf yucca, cane cholla, tree cholla, broom snakeweed, rubber rabbitbrush, and starvation prickly pear cactus abound here.

In another 0.1 mile or so, go right at the fork in the trail and look for the Old Faithful log lying prone, broken into several pieces. This huge tree was 194 feet tall and had a trunk diameter over 9 feet across. After admiring Old Faithful's giant remains, turn around and retrace your steps back to the main loop. Head right at the fork to continue counterclockwise. In several spots cement slab steps help hikers negotiate various ups and downs along the otherwise relatively flat trail. In another 0.1 mile you'll be back where you started at the trailhead behind the museum.

COLORADO

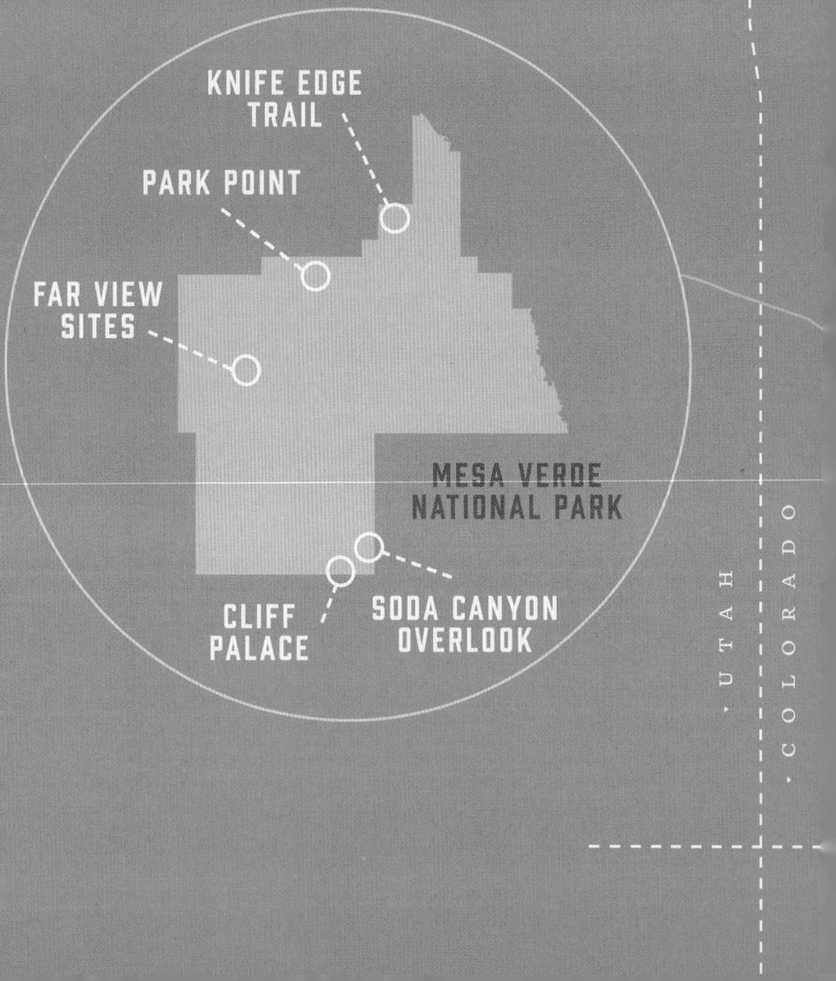

KNIFE EDGE
TRAIL

PARK POINT

FAR VIEW
SITES

MESA VERDE
NATIONAL PARK

CLIFF
PALACE

SODA CANYON
OVERLOOK

UTAH

COLORADO

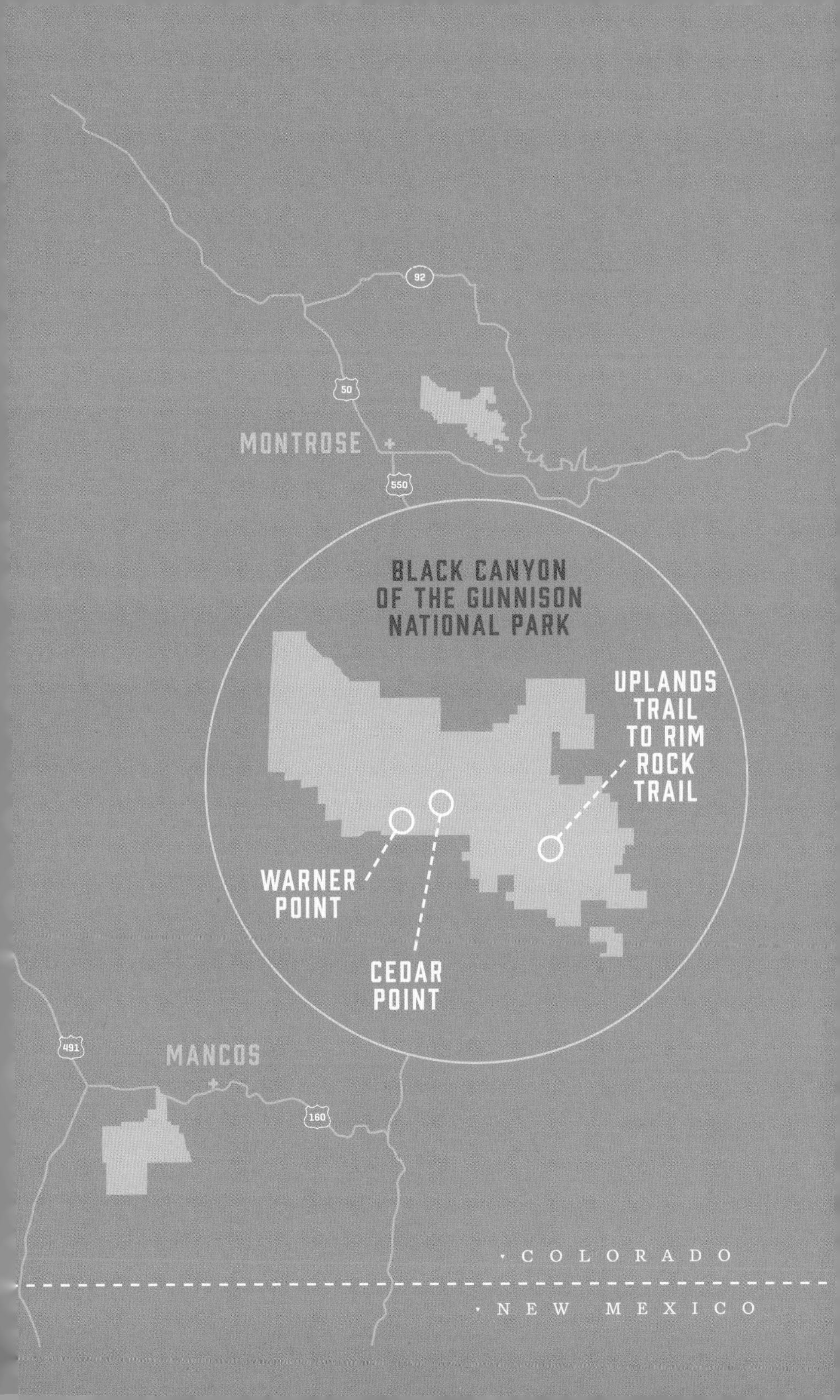

92

50

MONTROSE

550

BLACK CANYON
OF THE GUNNISON
NATIONAL PARK

UPLANDS
TRAIL
TO RIM
ROCK
TRAIL

WARNER
POINT

CEDAR
POINT

491

MANCOS

160

COLORADO

NEW MEXICO

FAR VIEW SITES

Tour aboveground dwellings of Ancestral Puebloans amidst wild overgrown natural beauty

DIFFICULTY
Easy

LOCATION
Chapin Mesa, west-central Mesa Verde

LENGTH
0.75 mile

WHEELCHAIR ACCESSIBLE
Yes, with assistance

PETS ALLOWED
No

The 0.75-mile loop hike around the Far View Sites showcases not just some of the original dwellings of Mesa Verde dating back to approximately 900 CE but also the profuse plant life and overall natural beauty of the region. The aboveground dwellings here are truly a marvel of human engineering and construction ingenuity from an age long before modern tools and machinery were available, but nature lovers will also find a lot to like hiking around this little mesa-top forest.

▾ Big sagebrush and pinyon pines line much of the sandy trail at the Far View Sites.

It's hard to believe that the Far View area was one of the most densely populated parts of the mesa from AD 900 to about AD 1300, when nearly 50 villages were crowded into an area just half a square mile. Stone foundations of some of the largest structures remain today and this short and flat hike takes you right by them.

▲ Coyote Village was home to dozens of Ancestral Puebloans beginning around 900 CE.

To get there from the Mesa Verde Visitor and Research Center off of U.S. Route 160 (US-160) in Mancos, Colorado, head west on Mesa Top Ruins Road and follow it for 17 miles as it zigs and zags its way south to the well-marked turnout for the Far View Sites on the left (east) side of the road.

Once you've parked the car, your first order of business should be checking out Far View House and Pipe Shrine House, two of the "ruins" here that are adjacent to the trailhead and parking area. These ancient aboveground dwellings were built more than 1100 years ago—predating the more famous cliff dwellings nearby by a century or more—by the Native American Ancestral Puebloans who lived here. (We know the age of the structures because archaeologists have used tree ring dating to determine exactly when the timbers used to bolster the floors and walls—long ago turned to charcoal but nevertheless bearing annual growth rings—were cut down.)

When it was built, Far View House, the largest structure remaining in the area to this day, was two stories tall and as such offered a commanding view out over the mesa, especially because the people living there had cut down most of the trees in and around the village sites. Today, just the bases and lower walls remain.

When you've poked around these two ruins to your heart's content, pick up the sandy dirt trail as it heads south for about 100 feet to Coyote Village where you can check out what remains of a small village site from 900 CE. Dozens of people lived in this compact complex of interconnected buildings including two large, underground circular rooms called kivas used for spiritual ceremonies.

Meanwhile, thriving populations of Utah junipers, pinyon pines, and other greenery do a great job hiding these and the other ruins here in the forest. This so-called pinyon-juniper woodland is also known as a "pygmy forest" since both tree species rarely exceed 30 feet in height. But just because the trees are relatively short doesn't mean they don't attain a ripe old age in many cases. Indeed, one particular "champion" Utah juniper here has been dated at more than 1300 years old.

Both trees also produce lots of seeds some years (a so-called "mast" crop) followed by three to six years of low seed production. Biologists consider this technique of mast seeding to be an evolutionary adaptation so that seed predators count on low seed counts every year and then are overwhelmed during masting years—and as such leave a lot of uneaten seeds behind that can germinate into a surge of saplings the next spring.

Another similarity between the junipers and pinyon pines here is the fact that they both reproduce by seed dispersal and are dependent on rodents, birds, and other wildlife to eat and then pass on their seeds via defecation. In fact, researchers have found that juniper berries that have passed through birds' digestive tracts germinate faster than uneaten seeds.

Below this vibrant pinyon-juniper canopy, a wide range of low-lying plants vies for water, sunlight, and whatever soil nutrients they can glean from the thin alkaline desert soils. Wildflowers abound in spring and early summer. Arrowleaf balsamroot blooms out in big floppy yellow flowers emerging from slender velvety green leaves. Dwarf larkspur sends up dainty shoots bearing violet-colored star-shaped flowers. Utah serviceberry grows in big bushes of almond-shaped green leaves with white flowers that look like caricatures of

Clockwise, from top left: Nineleaf biscuitroot

Utah serviceberry leafs out and blooms earlier than most other plants here and as such provides important forage for local mule deer hungry after a long winter.

The sunflower-shaped blooms of arrowleaf balsamroot come out in full force in spring and early summer.

stars. Nineleaf biscuitroot pops out a dozen or more little yellow flower heads that look like the finale of a fireworks show in miniature. Meanwhile, many of the usual suspects in terms of canyon country ground covers—big sagebrush, banana yucca, desert needlegrass, bitterbrush, rubber rabbitbrush, and bluebunch wheatgrass, among others—fill in the gaps.

Listen for the song and chatter of birds as you walk through the forest. Bewick's wrens, Townsend's solitaires, house finches, plumbeous vireos, blue-gray gnatcatchers, western tanagers, spotted towhees, Clark's nutcrackers, and three types of jays (Woodhouse's scrub, Steller's, and pinyon) are among the avian species that frequent this mesa-top woodland.

Sadly, an uptick in wildfires in recent years has degraded about half of the pinyon-juniper woodlands within Mesa Verde National Park. The most drastic of them was the

◂ Far View Tower and its keyhole-shaped kiva appear in a clearing in the pinyon-juniper forest.

Long Mesa Fire that scorched 2600 acres not far from here in July 2002 before monsoon rains put it out for good after a week-long burn. Decades of misguided fire suppression efforts had led to a situation where thick mats of kindling built up on the forest floor—so when a fire did start, it would burn hot and spread rapidly. But because of Yellowstone's summer of hell in 1988 and myriad other examples (including the Long Mesa burn), the National Park Service subsequently revamped its fire suppression regime to include hazard fuel reduction through thinning—that is, logging the small stuff and clearing debris from the forest floor, especially in and around developed areas and park infrastructure—and/or prescribed burns in more remote spots. With no kindling on the ground to burn, a lightning struck tree can't as easily start a fast-spreading wildfire. Hopefully this change will bear fruit in the coming years by sparing the rest of this already fragile pinyon-juniper woodland from obliteration.

From Coyote Village, the trail continues west and then north for about a quarter mile before hooking left (west) at the fork for a 0.1-mile detour to Megalithic House, another ruin from 1100 years ago that probably was a residence for a single family of status, although archaeologists still debate why the ancient Puebloans built it here. Megalithic House is the only ruin of the Far View Sites that is covered by a modern roof structure to protect its fragile excavations.

Head back to the main trail and you will soon come upon Far View Reservoir, which the Puebloans constructed as a water catchment system, as evidenced by pottery water jug shards and other clues found there. In another 0.1 mile you'll see Far View Tower, the remains of a small tower, perhaps used as a lookout back in the day, which abuts a single keyhole kiva. From here, it's another 0.1 mile back to the beginning of the loop and trailhead.

Walking around the Far View Sites is indeed the rare hike that combines natural scenic beauty with insights into human culture and civilization. While it might not be so easy to imagine yourself in the sandals of an Ancestral Puebloan, walking through their village sites immersed in this glorious pinyon-juniper woodland is a pretty good start.

MESA VERDE NATIONAL PARK

CLIFF PALACE

Drop down into an 800-year-old cliff dwelling complex to see how Ancestral Puebloans lived

DIFFICULTY
Easy to moderate

LOCATION
Chapin Mesa, Southwest Mesa Verde

LENGTH
0.25 mile

WHEELCHAIR ACCESSIBLE
No

PETS ALLOWED
No

Touring Cliff Palace is one of the iconic experiences of any visit to Mesa Verde National Park. The quarter-mile ranger-led "hike" gets you up close and personal with the cliff dwellers' homes here, carved out of an alcove along the side of Soda Canyon.

If you want to visit Cliff House, you must buy a $5 ticket in advance via the recreation.gov website or by calling 877-444-6777. Tickets are available fourteen days in advance on a rolling daily window. (For example, tickets for May 12 will be available starting April 28.) The tickets go quickly, so try to reserve them as soon as they become available online each day at 8 a.m. Mountain Time fourteen days before your planned visit date.

◂ The Ancestral Puebloans who built Cliff Palace and inhabited it for 800 years made their living by farming on the fertile mesa top above their unique dwellings.

To get there from the Mesa Verde Visitor and Research Center off of U.S. Route 160 (US-160) in Mancos, Colorado, head west on Mesa Top Ruins Road and follow it for 20.5 miles as it meanders mostly south and then turns left (east) onto the one-way Cliff Palace Loop. Go another 1.7 miles to the well-marked Cliff Palace trailhead. Park along either side of the one-way road; there are usually plenty of spots given that the departing tours are scheduled in advance and never overbooked.

▾ The round rooms in the cliff dwellings are called kivas and they were used for spiritual and political ceremonies.

Follow signs for the "Cliff Palace Tour" along a rough-hewn wooden fence to the marked meeting spot where the ranger will start the tour. Don't bring any food items or drinks (besides water) on the tour as even crumbs can attract rock squirrels and other wildlife that dig through the sand and cause unnecessary erosion. Also, kids must be big enough to negotiate ladders and uneven steps and terrain without being carried, and no pets are allowed. All in all, the walk through Cliff Palace is easy, although it does involve climbing four ladders, the highest of which is 12 feet tall.

After a short meet-and-greet, follow the ranger through a gate and down a set of two dozen metal stairs with railings on both sides. A large bigtooth maple tree spears out its loping limbs near the staircase. At the bottom of the metal stairs, continue further down into the canyon, first cutting between two tall sandstone fins and then negotiating some 60 sandstone steps of varying height made by the Civilian Conservation Corps back in the 1930s to ease access to the cliffside ruins. Use the railing along the left side as needed. The trail is shaded by the uphill slope for most of the way down, with occasional pinyon pine and Utah juniper trees providing additional coverage as they stretch out their twisted branches mostly along the downhill slope. Shrubby big sagebrush pops out of select niches along the way.

Down, down, down you go to the bottom of the alcove alongside Cliff Palace. From here, you'll have to climb up and into Cliff Palace from the north side. Ascend a rough-hewn eight-rung wooden ladder and emerge onto the level of Cliff Palace, which spreads out before you to the south. When the ranger says so, continue past a copse of small Gambel oaks framing the downslope, and the rock-borne cliffside village comes into full view. Continue up a few more sandstone steps into the edges of the structure.

Indeed, Cliff Palace is quite a sight. In its heyday, this alcove contained 150 rooms including 23 kivas used for spiritual ceremonies and other rites and gatherings. About 100 people lived here at any given time during the 750-plus years of human habitation. It was the largest of some 600 different cliff dwellings found throughout Mesa Verde National Park.

This and the other natural alcoves here and in the other surrounding canyons of Mesa Verde originated as seep springs in the sandstone canyon walls that naturally eroded out soft spots over hundreds of millennia. Because sandstone is porous, moisture seeps down through it. However, under the sandstone is a layer of shale that the moisture cannot penetrate. During winter, the moisture freezes and expands, cracking and loosening chunks of sandstone. These pieces later collapse, forming alcoves like the one

▲ The only way to visit Cliff House is to reserve a tour fourteen days in advance of your visit to Mesa Verde.

pictured. Most alcoves in Mesa Verde National Park are small crevices or ledges that can only accommodate a few small rooms. Only a few are large enough to house a dwelling the size of Cliff Palace.

It wasn't until 800-plus years ago—not even the blink of an eye in geological time—that humans began augmenting the alcoves with dwelling structures handcrafted from sandstone, mortar, and wood (for beams). The Ancestral Puebloans employed harder stones from nearby riverbeds to shape each sandstone block. They made mortar by mixing local soil with water and ash. Tiny pieces of stone, referred to as "chinking," were fitted into the mortar, filling the gaps and enhancing the structural stability of the walls. Many of the walls displayed a decorative layer of earthen plasters in various hues, including pink, brown, red, yellow, or white. Unfortunately for us, these plasters were among the first elements to erode over time.

The path leads south, giving visitors visibility into the size and scale of the various rooms, towers, and terraces that make up Cliff Palace. While the wooden beams and roofing structures the cliff dwellers used to provide protection from sun and the elements are long gone, it's easy to get a sense for what living here might be like just by looking at the structural skeletons of the place.

After centuries of living atop the mesa, the Ancestral Puebloans started moving down into newly carved homes in the natural alcoves of the cliffs around 1190 AD. They continued to grow corn, squash, and beans on the mesa top, which is blanketed with deposits of fertile red soil called loess. Blown in speck by speck by southwesterly winds over a span or more than a million years, the loess ranges from 3 to 30 feet deep and retains moisture, making it an ideal medium for agriculture.

The large pinyon pine and Utah juniper trees on the mesa are testament to the soil's fertility. Historians speculate that the logging of these trees for building and firewood may have degraded the land for agriculture to the point that the Ancestral Puebloans couldn't grow enough to sustain themselves. Others contend that a series of megadroughts across the region at the time stymied the cliff dwellers' agricultural efforts. Either way, these pioneering craftspeople felt compelled to move along to more fertile digs, abandoning their cliff dwellings altogether sometime before 1300 AD. It wasn't until 1888 that white settlers rediscovered Cliff Palace and the other cliff dwellings of Mesa Verde.

While Cliff Palace itself isn't the biggest draw for wildlife given the lack of plant life within the complex, rock squirrels, least chipmunks, and desert cottontails can sometimes be seen scurrying from rock to rock. Occasionally a mule deer passes through. Scan the skyline for white-throated swifts, which live in the canyon walls above and feed on insects and spiders that they eat during midair hunting forays. Meanwhile, turkey vultures, ever on the lookout for carrion from other animals' hunts, may ride air shafts high above the canyon.

Reptile lovers should keep an eye out for rock swifts. These little gray lizards—males have blue patches on either side of their bellies—are common in sloping and vertiginous sections of Mesa Verde like here at Cliff Palace. An evolutionary adaptation that has helped these little "brittle-tailed" lizards survive over the eons is their ability to break off (and regrow) their tails in the event a predator gets ahold of them. The predator only gets the end of a tail, while the

▸ Water from natural seeps in the sandstone has eroded out the alcove where Ancestral Puebloans built Cliff Palace; notice the greenery drinking it in right up against the bottom of the cliff dwellings.

lizard gets away. These and other lizards here play a vital role in keeping local insect population populations in check.

As you move through Cliff Palace, stick close to the ranger so you can learn as much as possible about various aspects of life there 800-plus years ago. Once the tour has had time to examine several different sections of the cliffside complex, follow the ranger up and out of the alcove and back up to the rim.

The short and easy adventure may be one of the most unique hikes you will ever take in a national park. While North America may technically be the "New World," the cliff dwellings at Mesa Verde prove that people have been here making a living out of nature for a very long time indeed.

MESA VERDE NATIONAL PARK

KNIFE EDGE TRAIL

Off-the-beaten-path green ridgeline hike showcases Mesa Verde's natural beauty and sweeping mountain vistas

DIFFICULTY
Easy

LOCATION
Northeast Mesa Verde

LENGTH
2 miles

WHEELCHAIR ACCESSIBLE
No

PETS ALLOWED
No

The 2-mile out-and-back hike along the Knife Edge in the northeastern section of Mesa Verde National Park gets you away from the crowds of the park's cliff dwellings and out onto a green ridge where the wonders of Mother Nature are the primary focus.

To get there from the Mesa Verde Visitor and Research Center off of U.S. Route 160 (US-160) in Mancos, Colorado, head west on Mesa Top Ruins Road and follow it for 4 miles before turning right (west) onto Navajo Road, which becomes Hopi Road after 0.1 mile at a fork. Here you'll continue straight ahead (technically taking the left branch of the fork, heading northwest). The well-marked Knife Edge parking lot and trailhead will be on the left (west) in 0.4 mile.

Start out hiking on the wide dirt trail, which came into existence more than a century ago as a roadbed but was closed to vehicular traffic in the 1930s due to the high costs of maintenance and the opening of a new park road nearby. Initially, the trail cuts through a notch between Prater Ridge on your left and Lone Cone to the right, with big sagebrush shrubs almost evenly spaced in the small flats in between. In about 0.2 mile, continue straight as the trail starts hugging

◂ Big sagebrush and other greenery proliferate on this hillside as Lone Cone vogues just to the north.

▸ Utah serviceberry forms dense thickets of leaves where it can grab a few square feet of desert floor to take root.

the north side of Prater Ridge. It's hard to believe that this stretch of trail was once wide and even enough to handle automobiles.

Keep hiking, enjoying the views down into the valley below. Pinyon pines and the occasional Utah juniper hang on at the fringes of Prater Ridge, while young Gambel oaks vie for sunlight and resources with lower lying shrubs. Meanwhile, Utah serviceberry, which has oval-shaped medium green leaves and blooms out in white flower stars in springtime, drapes itself over boulders and other spots where it can get a height boost and thus gather more sunlight.

Like elsewhere in the desert Southwest, spring and early summer is wildflower season here. Keep an eye out for the yellow blooms of flaxleaf mustard, which pop up by the dozen from a shag carpet of tall green stems and leaves. Parry's penstemon sports dainty violet miniblooms. Western blue virginsbower has huge floppy lavender blooms with yellow-green stigmas.

If you're lucky you may see a Chapin Mesa milkvetch, one of a handful of endemic plant species found only at Mesa Verde. These beauties grow to about 30 inches tall and sport unique green-white flowers. Other endemic plant species that can be found hereabouts include Cliff Palace milkvetch, Schmoll's milkvetch, Mesa Verde stickseed, and Mesa Verde wandering aletes.

As for wildlife, you could see a Rocky Mountain elk or mule deer, as well as a wide range of birds, including any number of different raptor species. Keep your eyes peeled on rocky uphill slopes for yellow-bellied marmots. Coyotes, mountain lions, and bobcats are no doubt lurking, but you may not see them. Rodents, bats, reptiles, and amphibians also make themselves at home here, but you're even less likely to see any of them.

Timing your hike for the late afternoon is ideal as the trail is

Below, from top: Parry's penstemon is one of several colorful blooms trailside here in late spring.

The blooms of western blue virginsbower, a member of the buttercup family, are a pleasant sight in late spring and early summer.

▲ Rubber rabbitbrush, one of the most widespread of all plants in the deserts of America, lines the trailside.

bathed in golden light then. Look for Sleeping Ute Mountain on the horizon to the west, and Totten Reservoir and Summit Lake beyond that even further in the distance.

After a mile of hiking, the trail comes to an abrupt end at a wooden National Park Service sign that simply says: "Stop!! Trail End—Slide Area." While the original road and trail kept going south for another mile until intersecting with the main park road at the Montezuma Overlook, falling rocks have forced the closure here to ensure visitor safety. So enjoy the view to the south from here that you weren't able to see along the hike and then turn around and retrace your steps (for another mile) back to the trailhead. Once you are back at your car, you'll appreciate how few other people you encountered on this seemingly forgotten yet astoundingly beautiful trek into the wilds of Mesa Verde National Park.

MESA VERDE NATIONAL PARK

SODA CANYON OVERLOOK

Trek through a classic western Colorado pinyon-juniper forest to a dizzying 1000-foot canyon drop-off overlook

	DIFFICULTY Easy
LOCATION Chapin Mesa, southwest Mesa Verde	LENGTH 1.2 miles
WHEELCHAIR ACCESSIBLE No	PETS ALLOWED No

The 1.2-mile out-and-back hike to the Soda Canyon Overlook zigzags through quintessential pinyon-juniper woodland to the rim of awe-inspiring Soda Canyon with views across to Balcony House, one of the most famous thirteenth-century cliff dwellings at Mesa Verde.

To get there from the Mesa Verde Visitor and Research Center off of U.S. Route 160 (US-160) in Mancos, Colorado, head west on Mesa Top Ruins Road and follow it for 20.4 miles as it meanders mostly south and then turns left (east) onto the one-way Cliff Palace Loop, which takes you another 3.9 miles to the well-marked Soda Canyon Overlook Trailhead. You can pull over along the side of the road nearby to park.

From the well-marked trailhead, follow the sandy dirt trail into the woods. Utah junipers and pinyon pines are everywhere, while stately ponderosa pines make occasional cameos with their signature jigsaw-style bark and sweet-smelling sap. Big sagebrush, bitterbrush, green ephedra, and other low-lying shrubs and herbs crowd the trailside and the spaces in between trees. Firecracker penstemon's red tubular flowers attract hummingbirds, moths,

◂ Cue the view of Soda Canyon: it's amazing what a small creek can do in terms of erosion if given a million years' time.

▸ A banana yucca grows out of a small soil patch on top of a long-ago fallen chunk of rock.

Clockwise, from top left: Firecracker penstemon and arrowleaf balsamroot add some welcome pops of color to the otherwise green-and-brown landscape.

Lobeleaf groundsel thrives in the arid conditions and poor soils of Mesa Verde.

The scarlet-red blooms of the claret cup cactus attract broad-billed, black-chinned, calliope, and rufous hummingbirds.

bees, and other pollinators. Watch where you step if you go off-trail, as you wouldn't want your foot to land on a starvation prickly pear cactus—or, even worse, a prairie rattlesnake.

After a half mile of hiking, you'll come to a fork for a small lollipop loop that takes you past three dramatic canyon overlook spots. Follow the sign left toward "Soda Canyon Overlook" and within a few more feet you'll be holding onto a railing on top of a metal fence keeping you from falling into the chasm below that is Soda Canyon. Hold on tight, catch your breath, and drink in the view that some say rivals the Grand Canyon in terms of natural beauty.

This 1000-foot-deep canyon was named for the white calcium carbonate deposits visible below the rim, which are the evaporative remains of seep springs once used by the cliff dwellers. Like the other canyons of Mesa Verde, this one developed along a fault line that hosted a stream that cut down into the soft sedimentary rock of the larger mesa over hundreds of millions of years. You can scroll through a geological timeline of the planet by analyzing the layers across the way in the canyon walls.

Move along to the second overlook, which has views of some small cliff house dwellings across the canyon. Spotting scopes help you zero in on details that are a quarter mile away and hard to see well with the naked eye. Then continue onto the third and final canyon overlook spot, which offers up views across to Balcony House.

The ancestors of today's Pueblo Indians carved and built this iconic cliff dwelling back in the thirteenth century to house as many as three dozen people in its 38 rooms (including two kivas, special round rooms dedicated to spiritual ceremonies). The residents farmed corn and other crops up above on the mesa top, which was covered in fertile volcanic loess soil, and got water from two nearby naturally occurring seep springs. While venturing down into Balcony House via a pre-booked paid tour with a National Park Service ranger is well worth the $4, the best view you'll get of this impressive cliff dwelling for free just may be here from the Soda Canyon Overlook—although you are a quarter mile away across the canyon.

When you've had your fill of Soda Canyon, follow the little loop back to the main trail and retrace your steps to the trailhead. The short hike packs a lot of bang for the buck with immersion in a pinyon-juniper forest and epic views down into a huge canyon with cliff dwellings as the cherry on top.

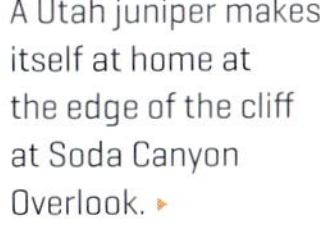

A Utah juniper makes itself at home at the edge of the cliff at Soda Canyon Overlook. ▸

MESA VERDE NATIONAL PARK

PARK POINT

Get an overview of Mesa Verde's sloping cuesta and natural setting from this high point at its north end

DIFFICULTY
Easy

LOCATION
North-central Mesa Verde

LENGTH
0.4 mile

WHEELCHAIR ACCESSIBLE
Yes, with assistance

PETS ALLOWED
Yes

The short walk out to Park Point is a great introduction to the natural setting of Mesa Verde in and of itself. Stopping there to take in the view of this 80-square-mile southwesterly sloping cuesta from its northeastern edge is a great way to get a sense of the context in which Ancestral Puebloans built their homes and made their living off the generous land some 800-plus years ago. (The 7-degree grade of the 80-square-mile Mesa Verde plateau makes it a *cuesta*, not a true *mesa*, which would be flatter.) While there are no ruins or cliff dwellings to ogle at Park Point—the only human-built structure up there these days is the fire lookout cabin—views of wildflowers and forested ridges as far as the eye can see are entertainment enough.

▾ The "trail" at Park Point is actually more of a wide, paved pathway navigable by foot or wheelchair.

To get there from the Mesa Verde Visitor and Research Center off U.S.

▲ You can see for hundreds of miles in every direction on a clear day at Park Point.

Route 160 (US-160) in Mancos, Colorado, head west on Mesa Top Ruins Road and follow it as it meanders south and then west for 10.4 miles to the well-marked turnout for Park Point. Turn right (north) and follow until it dead-ends at the circular Park Point parking area.

Park the car and set out on foot on the paved pathway uphill to Park Point. Immediately your view opens up in every direction and you feel like you could take off on the breeze and fly to neighboring ridges. But keep those feet on the ground and keep walking. In a few hundred feet go right at the fork and check out the cute and rustic fire lookout cabin.

Built in 1939 by the Civilian Conservation Corps, with an octagonal design reminiscent of a Navajo hogan, it sits at the highest elevation in the park at 8572 feet above sea level. By the 1950s there were more than 8000 such fire lookout cabins scattered across the United States, many in national parks, which played a vital role in the early detection of wildfires. But over time newer technologies, including fire detection by aircraft, rendered many of them obsolete. Fortunately, state and federal agencies and organizations like the National Forest Fire Lookout Association have made efforts to restore some of these historic lookouts, including

▲ The perennially snow-capped San Juan Mountains lie some 70 miles "as the eagle flies" north of Mesa Verde's Park Point.

the Park Point Lookout here, which is now listed on the National Register of Historic Places.

The 360-degree view from the deck of the fire lookout, and pretty much everywhere else at Park Point, takes in the jagged snow-capped peaks of the San Juan Mountains, including several "fourteeners" (mountains topping 14,000 feet in elevation), to the north, the high desert canyonlands of New Mexico to the south, Sleeping Ute Mountain to the west, and the La Plata Mountains to the east.

Continue past the lookout to a small viewpoint. If you've never been to Mesa Verde, consider this view to the south across the sloping cuesta a preview of things to come. Turn around and retrace your steps past the fire lookout and then continue onto the path as it forks right (north) following the ridgeline of the small canyon to the north. In another 0.1 mile you'll reach a fenced-off viewpoint area, which is a great spot to watch the sunset.

Looking south over the verdant cuesta, it's no wonder that it's named the "Green Table" (Mesa Verde). A verdant landscape rolls away from you punctuated by a surprising diversity of plant life given the ecosystem is a high, dry desert. Mountain mahogany, pinyon pine, Utah juniper, and Gambel oak punctuate the slopes all around, with big sagebrush, bitterbrush, and Utah serviceberry filling in the gaps, keeping things green.

If it's spring or early summer, blooming wildflowers will be everywhere. Arrowleaf balsamroot's aggregation of leathery green leaves support a dozen or so floppy yellow blooms that seem to stand at attention for passing hikers. Evening primrose and Indian paintbrush lend occasional splashes of color to the otherwise green landscape. If you venture off-trail, watch where you step, as starvation prickly pear cacti grow close to the ground and blend in well with their surroundings, except when they bloom out in paper thin yellow or violet flowers.

As for wildlife, mule deer and wild turkey are relatively common around these parts, but there are a lot of other creatures out and about that you probably won't see. Coyotes, American black bears, Rocky Mountain elk, mountain lions, red foxes, and golden-mantled ground squirrels are just a few of the mammalian species surely roaming not far from where you stand. Meanwhile, reptiles are well-represented here by four species of lizard—collared lizards, six-lined racerunners, short-horned lizards, and northern plateau lizards—and three types of snakes—bullsnakes, yellow-bellied racers, and prairie rattlesnakes.

▾ Bitterbrush is one of several desert plants that flourish up here in the fertile loess on top of Mesa Verde's cuesta.

As for birds, upwards of 200 different avian species call the park home or visit for extended seasonal periods. Bird-watchers love Park Point as it's a good spot to see songbirds—mountain bluebirds, black-capped chickadees, red-winged blackbirds, pine siskins—flitting between trees as well as raptors—golden eagles, peregrine falcons, American kestrels—overhead on the aerial hunt. And if you hear some repetitive drumming coming from the forest nearby, it's likely the sound of a hairy woodpecker searching for beetle larvae and other delicacies in the bark of a tree. While you're less likely to encounter wildlife at a crowded viewpoint area like Park Point, venturing out for hikes in lesser visited sections of the national park can increase your chances of encountering wild animals in their own habitat.

Surveying the scene from here, it's easy to understand why the Ancestral Puebloans who built their homes in the nearby cliff alcoves would want to call this area home. When you've soaked in the sights, sounds, and smells of elemental nature enough at this Eden-like setting here atop Park Point, turn around and retrace your steps back to the parking area, your spirit buoyed no doubt by the experience.

From top: Seeing the tall, floppy yellow blooms of arrowleaf balsamroot is always a pleasure.

The Fire Lookout at Park Point was built in 1939 by the Civilian Conservation Corps, a New Deal program by the federal government to get Americans back to work during the Great Depression.

BLACK CANYON OF THE GUNNISON NATIONAL PARK

UPLANDS TRAIL TO RIM ROCK TRAIL

Traverse through Gambel oak woodland to gobsmacking views of Black Canyon of the Gunnison

DIFFICULTY
Easy to moderate

LOCATION
Southeast Black Canyon

LENGTH
2.8 miles

WHEELCHAIR ACCESSIBLE
No

PETS ALLOWED
No*

This iconic loop hike crosses through a classic desert highlands Gambel oak forest and out onto the rim of the Black Canyon of the Gunnison for otherworldly views into and across one of America's great chasms. This national park's namesake canyon walls are black only because they are so vertical that they are almost always in the dark shadows. If you have time for one short hike in the national park here, make it the Uplands Trail to Rimrock Trail Loop.

To get there from Montrose, Colorado, head east on U.S. Route 50 (US-50) for 5.8 miles, then turn left to head north on Colorado State Route 347 (CO-347) for 5.2 miles, where the road enters Black Canyon of the Gunnison National Park and becomes Rim Drive Road. Follow it for another 1.7 miles and park at or near the South Rim Visitor Center.

When you've got your hiking boots or trail shoes on, head down behind the visitor center and out to Gunnison

*Pets not allowed, except on Rimrock Trail on leash

Point, which sits on an outcrop jutting out into the canyon, to take in the spectacular Black Canyon view. Look down to see the ribbonlike Gunnison River still cutting its way through the canyon a third of a mile below you.

▲ A Utah juniper snag hangs out on the South Rim of Black Canyon. Note the other side of the canyon .75 mile to the east.

The story of the Black Canyon's formation starts about 60 million years ago when a small area of land here uplifted due to tectonic shifting, bringing 1.8 billion-year-old metamorphic rock to high elevations. Then about 30 million years ago, large volcanoes erupted on either side of this so-called Gunnison Uplift, burying it in volcanic ash and sediments that over millions of years lithified into rock. Then, around 2 million years ago, the Gunnison River began flowing in force, over time eroding all of the volcanic rock and cutting a deep canyon in the metamorphic rock below, resulting in the dark and narrow canyon below you today. The canyon is even steep at its bottom, where the Gunnison River drops an average of 43 feet per mile—and 240 feet per mile at its steepest point below Chasm View some 2.3 miles to the northwest of Gunnison Point.

When you've contemplated the chasm to your heart's content from the overlook at Gunnison Point, backtrack

Gambel oaks stretch out their boughs to welcome you to the Uplands Trail. ▸

to where you started behind the visitor center and pick up the well-marked Oak Flat Trail. Go left at the first fork and climb gently over rough terrain through a forest of short Gambel oak trees before turning left again onto the well-marked Uplands Trail.

Colorado's most abundant and widespread of three oak species, the Gambel oaks all around you are true survivors—they can tolerate rocky soils, high winds, heavy snow, wildfire, and drought thanks to deep roots and "xeromorphic" leaves, which are able to store water to make it through dry periods. Connecting the tree's roots to its trunk just below the surface is a rounded woody mass called a lignotuber, which contains masses of buds and food reserves that the tree can also draw on in lean times. As a result of these evolutionary adaptations, Gambel oaks are able to sprout new trunks and form colonies easily, just like here at Oak Flat.

While you're here amidst the Gambels, stop for a minute or two and listen and observe—you may just be lucky enough to hear or see some wildlife. Local mule deer can browse on the Gambels' twigs to help sustain them during cold, dark winters when other food sources aren't available, and a wide variety of mammals and birds collects and caches the trees' autumn acorns. Meanwhile, long-tailed weasels are right at home prowling for small mammals throughout the oak flat here. And desert cottontail rabbits rustle through dense stands of sagebrush in search of grasses and shoots.

Above, from left: These western tent caterpillars will turn into moths within six weeks; their tents don't harm the host plant.

Pinyon pine is one of the more common trees here at Black Canyon of the Gunnison.

As for birds, you can often hear the songs and chatter of spotted towhees, western tanagers, black-throated gray warblers, blue-gray gnatcatchers, and black-headed grosbeaks as they flit among the oaks. And butterfly lovers will rejoice at the sight of Colorado hairstreaks. The larvae of these iridescent purple-black-and-rust-colored beauties feed only on the leaves of Gambel oaks, while adult hairstreaks get most of their nutrition from the Gambels' sap and also the sweet liquid exuding from insect "galls" that form on some of the trees when oak gall wasps lay their eggs inside the bark, swelling small sections of the tree's trunk.

Keep hiking as the Uplands Trail crosses the main park road and ascends gently through the Gambels interspersed with healthy doses of big sagebrush filling in the gaps on the sandy desert floor. The trail curves left across a seasonal creek and then crosses the park road again, intersecting with Rimrock Trail. Turn left (west) and follow Rimrock Trail for 0.8 mile as it loops you back to the visitor center.

While you definitely need to watch your step here, the trail is well maintained and typically built back from any steep overhangs. Looking east from here, the other side of the Black Canyon is more than 0.75 mile away. Lots of boulder chunks have fallen off nearby hillsides and rolled into place here and there, collecting lichens that derive nutrients from their rock host's substrate as well as the passing breeze.

Pinyon pines stand straight and tall, while ponderosa pines and Utah junipers occupy the occasional cliff edge. If you're here in spring or early summer, enjoy the color

Short-styled bluebells are among the spring wildflowers you can spy along Uplands and Rimrock trails. ▸

display from a profusion of wildflowers taking advantage of the lack of tree canopy as they soak up the sun at the canyon edge. Big yellow floppy blooms of arrowleaf balsamroot punctuate the trailside. Delicate little star-shaped violet blooms of spreading phlox are easily trampled underfoot, while twolobe larkspur sports large star-shaped purple flowers that can branch up and out to human eye level. The daisy-shaped yellow blooms of lambstongue ragwort stand up on their own in small groupings of a half dozen or so plants. And the blooms of short-styled bluebells look like purple and blue fireworks shooting down on the Fourth of July.

Between the canyon views to the east and floral diversity to the west, there is indeed a lot of eye candy along this short stretch of trail. Make sure to watch your step as the trail, although relatively flat, is rough with lots of rocks and roots as impediments. After passing Tomichi Point, where cliff-edge canyon views abound, finish the hike with a gradual descent to the visitor center where you started some 2.8 miles ago.

Black Canyon of the Gunnison may be a lesser known national park, and those who visit may just want to keep it that way. Indeed, the lack of crowds, immersion in elemental nature, and awe-inspiring views here along the Uplands to Rimrock loop are as good as it gets in Southwest canyon country.

BLACK CANYON OF THE GUNNISON NATIONAL PARK

CEDAR POINT

Short woodland jaunt leads to the Painted Wall and deepest Black Canyon views

	DIFFICULTY Easy
LOCATION North-central Black Canyon	LENGTH 0.4 mile
WHEELCHAIR ACCESSIBLE No	PETS ALLOWED On leash

The Cedar Point Nature Trail hike may be short, but it cuts through a quintessential pinyon-juniper woodland to an overlook with spectacular views into and across the deepest, steepest, narrowest canyon in North America.

To get there from Montrose, Colorado, head east on U.S. Route 50 (US-50) for 5.8 miles, then turn left to head north on Colorado State Route 347 (CO-347) for 5.2 miles, where the road enters Black Canyon of the Gunnison National Park and becomes Rim Drive Road. Follow it for another 5.9 miles and pull over in one of the dozen or so parking spots along the west side of the road. Pets are allowed on leash.

The short walk on a relatively level dirt trail traverses a quarter mile through the cliffside woodland dominated by pinyon pines and Utah junipers. Some other trees making cameos here include Gambel oak, mountain mahogany, single-leaf ash, and Rocky Mountain juniper, which may not look very old but can live 800-plus years out here on the edge of the canyon.

The understory is dominated by big sagebrush, Indian ricegrass, and big spreading clumps of Utah serviceberry with its signature white flowers in springtime. Arrowleaf balsamroot's twisty leathery green leaves provide a strong base for huge floppy yellow springtime blooms. Thicksepal cryptantha features white rounded star-shaped blooms with yellow and black stigmas that lend it the nickname "cat's eye." Occasional white and yellow Eaton's daisies peek through violet carpets of spreading phlox blooms. Silky lupine helps convert airborne nitrogen into nutrients that other plants can use below the surface as fertilizer. The plant's distinctive green star-shaped leaves send up climbing blue-purple blooms in early summer.

◂ The Painted Wall, where one form of molten volcanic rock squeezed through fissures in the darker substrate millions of years ago, is the most photographed feature at Black Canyon of the Gunnison National Park.

As for wildlife, if you hear a singsongy witch's cackle, look around for a pinyon jay. These small dusky blue corvids (related to crows, ravens, and other jays) are codependent on the pinyon pine trees so common around these parts, eating and also caching large numbers of the plant's nutritious seeds, which are similar to the pine nuts we buy as delicacies at the grocery store. Some of these wild caches are abandoned or otherwise forgotten—and as a result spring to life as new pinyon pine shoots several months later when the weather warms up.

Another bird you might see around here, especially in flight above the canyon, is the white-throated swift. These striking black-and-white birds seem to defy physics as they dive, twist, and turn midair in order to hunt their prey, airborne insects, while on the wing. Hundreds of the little avian athletes live in colonies in the crevices in the walls of the Black Canyon, using their saliva to glue small nests of twigs and moss to the nearly vertical walls.

As for mammals, coyotes, red foxes, and ringtails tend to stay out of sight during the day, but you may get lucky and see one on the hunt. A variety of rodents—pinyon mice, least chipmunks, rock squirrels—goes about their business in the trees and on and below the forest floor. Mule deer and Rocky Mountain elk sometimes pass through, browsing on fresh green shoots in spring and summer and oak twigs, Utah serviceberry leaves, and big sagebrush branches in the colder months. And occasionally Rocky Mountain bighorn sheep have been seen around these parts munching on the nutritious shoots of Indian ricegrass between forays out onto the steep canyon walls below.

Keep moving through this dense and diverse forest and within just a quarter mile you'll be at the overlook. Watch your step and keep a hand on small children as only a couple of rough-hewn wooden fence rails will keep you from falling into the Black Canyon itself. Indeed, it's about an 1800-foot drop from here to the bottom where the Gunnison River is still eroding its way deeper and deeper into the earth.

Looking directly across the canyon to the northwest, it's a half mile to the other side from here. Below the opposite rim is the Painted Wall, named for the jagged off-white lines seemingly scrawled or painted horizontally across the brown-black canyon walls. These lighter colored lines show where pegmatite, a form of molten volcanic rock, squeezed its way through fissures in the otherwise dark-colored rock of the canyon walls. The Painted Wall is actually the highest cliff in Colorado, measuring some 2300 feet—almost double

Opposite, clockwise, from top: Rocky Mountain junipers are some of the longest living organisms in Southwest canyon country, with an average lifespan of 600 to 800 years.

Thicksepal cryptantha is known as "cat's eye" because of its distinctive stigma shape.

Indian paintbrush is one of the most common wildflowers across the West.

the height of the 102-story Empire State Building!—from the rim to the canyon floor.

When you've had enough of the view, turn around and retrace your steps back to the parking area. The total hiking distance is less than a half mile, but in terms of bang for the buck, the Cedar Point Nature Trail is hard to beat.

BLACK CANYON OF THE GUNNISON NATIONAL PARK

WARNER POINT

Cut through pinyon-juniper forest primeval to red rock skyline and Black Canyon views

DIFFICULTY	
	Easy to moderate

LOCATION	LENGTH
Northwest Black Canyon	1.5 miles
WHEELCHAIR-ACCESSIBLE	**PETS ALLOWED**
No	No

The 1.5-mile out-and-back hike to Warner Point gives nature lovers a good sense of the pinyon-juniper forest here at the edge of the Black Canyon, elevation 8000-plus feet, capped off with astonishing views down into and across Colorado's most famous chasm.

To get there from Montrose, Colorado, head east on U.S. Route 50 (US-50) for 5.8 miles then turn left to head north on Colorado State Route 347 (CO-347) for 5.2 miles, where the road enters Black Canyon of the Gunnison National Park and becomes Rim Drive Road. Follow it for another 7.7 miles until it dead-ends at High Point, where a circular parking area and turnaround accommodate about two dozen cars.

Silky lupine is a hardy early colonizer, which helps make the soil more fertile for other plants around it. ▾

Take in the view to the south of the canyon from High Point and then walk to the well-marked Warner Point trailhead and enter the pinyon-juniper woodland. The well-maintained dirt

▲ Arrowleaf balsamroot's yellow flowers decorate the trailside on the way to Warner Point.

trail follows a ridgeline out into the Black Canyon. While the destination of Warner Point is only about 20 feet below the trailhead in elevation, the ridgeline hike crosses over a saddle in the middle of its .75-mile run, so the total elevation gain and loss is approximately 425 feet. The steeper sections of trail are augmented by stone-and-log stair trestles to make the up-and-down easier. Several benches along the way beckon hikers to rest awhile and enjoy the views.

Pinyon pines and Utah junipers are the dominant tree species here in this cozy little woodland, but a few Rocky Mountain junipers, Gambel oaks, ponderosa pines, desert mountain mahoganies, and even some Douglas firs poke their way into the canopy as well. Lower to the ground, big sagebrush and Utah serviceberry are omnipresent, while foxtail barley, needle-and-thread, and Indian ricegrass prevail where they can.

Of course, a range of wildflowers keeps things interesting, especially in spring and early summer. One of these early season bloomers is silky lupine, which features climbing five-petaled lavender-blue flowers evolved perfectly to

A Douglas fir and pinyon pine are neighbors on the edge of the Black Canyon.

enclose visiting bees on the hunt for nectar. But silky lupine punches above its ecological weight in more ways than one. Indeed, this pea-relative legume takes nitrogen from the air and converts it into a chemical substance underground that makes the soil more nutritious for all of the surrounding plants. These lupines are well adapted to the sandy soils here in the high desert, with long, deep taproots that help them survive forest fires. Indeed, they are typically some of the first spiky new shoots to re-emerge in the soil in spring following a burn. Twolobe larkspur, Indian paintbrush, short-styled bluebell, and arrowleaf balsamroot are among the other common wildflowers here.

As for fauna, wild turkey and mule deer are probably the most often sighted species around these parts, but the most famous may just be the Gunnison sage grouse, which was listed in 2014 as a threatened species by the U.S. Fish & Wildlife Service under the Endangered Species Act. Similar to but much rarer than its close relative the greater sage grouse, both birds share the same spectacular courtship routine, whereby the males gather on "lekking grounds"—spots in the forest they have reserved for mating rituals—puffing themselves up while fanning their tails into starbursts and using pouches in their chests to make strange bubbling, gurgling sounds. Meanwhile, the females gather in flocks to watch the unusual displays and pick their mates accordingly, going on to raise the young entirely on their own. (Some guys have all the luck.)

The federal government has hedged on listing the greater sage grouse as threatened or endangered due to political blowback from western landowners irate about "government overreach"—but only 150,000 or so of the iconic western birds are left across its eight-state range in the Great Basin of the American West. Meanwhile, less than 4000 of the "threatened" Gunnison sage grouse are left in the wild across small sections of western Colorado and eastern Utah, and the bird remains threatened as its population is still declining. Consider yourself lucky if you get to see one of Gunnison's iconic black-and-white fowl, although you are definitely in the right place for a sighting.

More wildlife to keep an eye out for on the way to and from Warner Point includes white-throated swifts, pinyon jays, Clark's nutcrackers, golden eagles, Rocky Mountain

▸ The U.S. Fish and Wildlife Service listed the Gunnison sage grouse as threatened in 2014, but its population numbers have only decreased since then.

elk, mountain lions, black bears, coyotes, least chipmunks, porcupines, and golden-mantled ground squirrels, among others.

Keep walking and enjoy the panorama. Even though the hike is through the trees, you are at the pinnacle of a ridgeline, so views abound in every direction. If it's a clear day, you'll have no trouble seeing 14,150-foot Mount Sneffels and its neighboring "fourteeners" (14,000-plus-foot peaks) in the San Juan range about 40 miles away to the south as the eagle flies. Look east for views of the West Elk Mountains, which are 30 miles away but feel like you could reach out and touch them. Likewise, it seems like you could bound down into the Uncompahgre Valley and the city of Montrose off to the southwest, but it's actually 10 miles away.

After 0.75 mile of up and down ridgeline hiking, you'll come to Warner Point itself, where the overlooks offer views down into and across the Black Canyon. About 1.5 miles separates the east side of the canyon where you're standing from the west side, and it's a half mile down from the tip of Warner Point to the bottom of the canyon. Indeed, you are living on the edge as you peer down into the dark and foreboding chasm below you.

When you've had enough of this look down into the dark void of the canyon, turn around and retrace your steps back to the trailhead and parking area, content that you have experienced the best the Black Canyon of the Gunnison National Park has to offer.

LIST OF SPECIES

Trees

Alderleaf mountain mahogany (*Cercocarpus montanus*)
Bigtooth maple (*Acer grandidentatum*)
Box elder (*Acer negundo*)
Desert mountain mahogany (*Cercocarpus ledifolius*)
Fremont cottonwood (*Populus fremontii*)
Gambel oak (*Quercus gambelii*)
Great Basin bristlecone pine (*Pinus longaeva*)
New Mexico locust (*Robinia neomexicana*)
Pinyon pine (*Pinus edulis*)
Ponderosa pine (*Pinus ponderosa*)
Quaking aspen (*Populus tremuloides*)
Rocky Mountain juniper (*Juniperus scopulorum*)
Rocky Mountain white oak (*Quercus utahensis*)
Single-leaf ash (*Fraxinus anomala*)
Single-leaf pinyon (*Pinus monophyla*)
Subalpine fir (*Abies lasiocarpa*)
Tree cholla (*Cylindropuntia imbricata*)
Utah juniper (*Juniperus osteosperma*)
Velvet ash (*Fraxinus velutina*)
Water birch (*Betula occidentalis*)
Western juniper (*Juniperus occidentalis*)
White fir (*Abies concolor*)

Shrubs and Vines

Alkali jimmyweed (*Isocoma acradenia*)
Apache plume (*Fallugia paradoxa*)
Arizona cliffrose (*Purshia subintegra*)
Beavertail prickly pear cactus (*Opuntia basilaris*)
Big sagebrush (*Artemesia tridentata*)
Bitterbrush (*Purshia tridentata*)
Black sagebrush (*Artemisia nova*)
Blackbrush (*Coleogyne ramosissima*)
Broom snakeweed (*Gutierrezia sarothrae*)
California brickelbush (*Brickellia californica*)
Cane cholla (*Cylinidroppuntia imbricata*)
Canyon grape (*Vitis arizonica*)
Claret cup cactus (*Echinocereus triglochidiatus*)
Cliff fendlerbush (*Fendlera rupicola*)
Creeping barberry (*Mahonia repens*)
Deer goldenbush (*Ericameria parryi*)
Desert willow (*Chilopsis linearis*)
Fernbush (*Chamaebatiaria millefolium*)
Fragrant sumac (*Rhus aromatica*)
Fremont barberry (*Berberis fremontii*)
Green rabbitbrush (*Chrysothamnus viscidiflorus*)

Greenleaf manzanita (*Arctostaphylos patula*)
Kanab yucca (*Yucca angustissima* var. *kanabensis*)
Littleleaf mountain mahogany (*Cercocarpus intricatus*)
Narrowleaf yucca (*Yucca angustissima*)
Notch-leaf scorpionweed (*Heliotrope phacelia*)
Parish's goldeneye (*Bahiopsis parishii*)
Prickly pear cactus (*Opuntia* spp.)
Roundleaf buffaloberry (*Shepherdia rotundifolia*)
Rubber rabbitbrush (*Chrysothamnus nauseosus*)
Sand sagebrush (*Artemisia filifolia*)
Shadescale saltbush (*Atriplex confertifolia*)
Sonoran scrub oak (*Quercus turbinella*)
Stansbury cliffrose (*Purshia stansburiana*)
Torrey's jointfir (*Ephedra torreyana*)
Utah serviceberry (*Amelanchier utahensis*)
Wax currant (*Ribes cereum*)
Western serviceberry (*Amelanchier alnifolia*)
Winterfat (*Krascheninnikovia lanata*)
Woolly locoweed (*Astragalus mollissimus*)

Herbaceous Plants

Alkali sacaton (*Sporobolus airoides*)
Arizona thistle (*Cirsium arizonicum*)
Arrowleaf balsamroot (*Balsamorhiza sagittata*)
Banana yucca (*Yucca baccata*)
Blowout grass (*Redfieldia flexuosa*)
Bluebunch wheatgrass (*Pseudoroegneria spicata*)
Blue grama (*Bouteloua gracilis*)
Bottlebrush squirreltail (*Elymus elymoides*)
Bryce Canyon paintbrush (*Castilleja revealii*)
Canada thistle (*Cirsium arvense*)
Canadian lousewort (*Pedicularis canadensis*)
Canaigre dock (*Rumex hymenosepalus*)
Canyonlands hymenoxys, or Ives' four-nerved daisy (*Tetraneuris acaulis*)
Cardinal monkeyflower (*Mimulus cardinalis*)
Chaparral (*Larrea tridentata*)
Chapin Mesa milkvetch (*Astragalus schmolliae*)
Cheatgrass (*Bromus tectorum*)
Clasping pepperweed (*Lepidium perfoliatum*)
Cliff Palace milkvetch (*Astragalus deterior*)
Colorado columbine (*Aquilegia caerulea*)
Common dandelion (*Taraxacum officinale*)
Common dogbane (*Apocynum cannabinum*)

Common peppergrass (*Lepidium densiflorum*)
Crispleaf buckwheat (*Eriogonum corymbosum*)
Crucifixion thorn (*Canotia holacantha*)
Dainty Nuttall's gilia (*Linanthastrum nuttallii*)
Death camas (*Zigadenus venenosus*)
Desert dandelion (*Malacothrix glabrata*)
Desert four o'clock (*Mirabilis multiflora*)
Desert globemallow (*Sphaeralcea ambigua*)
Desert needlegrass (*Pappostipa speciosa*)
Desert paintbrush (*Castilleja chromosa*)
Desert phlox (*Phlox austromontana*)
Desert prince's plume (*Stanleya pinnata*)
Desert sand verbena (*Abronia villosa*)
Desert wirelettuce (*Stephanomeria runcinate*)
Desert wishbone-bush (*Mirabilis laevis*)
Desert globe mallow (*Sphaeralcea ambigua*)
Dropseed (*Sporobolus spp.*)
Dwarf larkspur (*Delphinium nuttallianum*)
Dwarf lupine (*Lupinus pusillus*)
Eaton's daisy (*Erigeron eatonii*)
Elkweed (*Frasera speciosa*)
Firecracker penstemon (*Penstemon eatonii*)
Flatspine bur ragweed (*Ambrosia acanthicarpa*)
Flaxleaf mustard (*Camelina microcarpa*)
Foster's columbine (*Aquilegia fosteri*)
Four-wing saltbush (*Atriplex canescens*)
Foxtail barley (*Hordeum jubatum*)
Fragrant evening primrose (*Oenothera cespitosa*)
Fringe-leaf necklacepod (*Sophora stenophylla*)
Golden columbine (*Aquilegia chrysantha*)
Golden crownbeard (*Verbesina encelioides*)
Gooseberry (*Ribes hirtellum*)
Green ephedra (*Ephedra viridis*)
Hairy false goldenaster (*Heterotheca villosa*)
Harriman's yucca (*Yucca harrimaniae*)
Hispid goldenaster (*Heterotheca subaxillaris*)
Hoary tansyaster (*Machaeranthera canescens*)
Idaho fescue (*Festuca idahoensis*)
Indian paintbrush (*Castilleja linariifolia*)
Indian ricegrass (*Achnatherum hymenoides*)
Intermountain bitterweed (*Hymenoxys helenioides*)
Jimsonweed (*Datura wrightii*)
Kentucky bluegrass (*Poa pratensis*)
Lambstongue ragwort (*Senecio integerrimus*)
Lobeleaf groundsel (*Senecio multilobatus*)
Meadow fescue (*Festuca pratensis*)
Mesa Verde stickseed (*Hackelia gracilenta*)
Mesa Verde wandering aletes (*Aletes macdougalii*)
Miner's lettuce (*Montia perfoliate*)

Mormon tea, or green ephedra (*Ephedra viridis*)
Mountain mahogany (*Cercocarpus montanus*)
Mullein (*Verbascum thapsus*)
Musk thistle (*Carduus nutans*)
Muttongrass (*Poa fendleriana*)
Navajo fleabane (*Erigeron nanus*)
Needle and thread (*Hesperostipa comata*)
Nineleaf biscuitroot (*Lomatium triternatum*)
Ocotillo (*Fouquieria splendens*)
Pale evening primrose (*Oenothera pallida*)
Palmer's penstemon (*Penstemon palmeri*)
Panamint cryptantha (*Cryptantha angustifolia*)
Parry's penstemon (*Penstemon parryi*)
Plateau penstemon (*Penstemon scariosus*)
Prairie sunflower (*Helianthus petiolaris*)
Purple three-awn (*Aristida purpurea*)
Rose heath (*Rhododendron macrophyllum*)
Rough mule's ears (*Wyethia scabra*)
Russian thistle (*Salsola kali*)
Salt heliotrope (*Heliotropium curassavicum*)
Sandreed (*Calamovilfa longifolia*)
Scarlet globemallow (*Sphaeralcea coccinea*)
Schmoll's milkvetch (*Astragalus schmolliae*)
Sego lily (*Calochortus nuttallii*)
Silky lupine (*Lupinus sericeus*)
Small-flower fishhook cactus (*Sclerocactus parviflorus*)
Smallflower globemallow (*Sphaeralcea parvifolia*)
Smooth brome (*Bromus inermis*)
Sneezeweed (*Helenium autumnale*)
Sonoran scrub oak (*Quercus turbinella*)
Southern maidenhair fern (*Adiantum capillus-veneris*)
Specklepod milkvetch (*Astragalus lentiginosus*)
Spineless horsebrush (*Tetradymia canescens*)
Spreading phlox (*Phlox diffusa*)
Stemless four-nerved daisy (*Tetraneuris acaulis*)
Stonecrop, or spearleaf stonecrop (*Sedum lanceolatum*)
Stream orchid (Epipactis gigantea)
Tall-fringed bluebells (*Mertensia ciliata*)
Tansyleaf tansyaster (*Machaeranthera tanacetifolia*)
Tarragon (*Artemisia dracunculus* var. *glauca*)
Thickleaf penstemon (*Penstemon pachyphyllus*)
Thicksepal cryptantha (*Cryptantha crassipes*)
Tufted evening primrose (*Oenothera caespitosa*)
Tulip prickly pear cactus (*Opuntia phaeacantha* var. *major*)
Twolobe larkspur (*Delphinium nuttallianum*)
Utah agave (*Agave utahensis*)
Utah daisy (*Erigeron utahensis*)
Utah penstemon (*Penstemon utahensis*)
Watercress (*Nasturtium officinale*)
Welsh's milkvetch (*Asclepius welshii*)
Western blue virginsbower (*Clematis occidentalis*)

Western columbine (*Aquilegia formosa*)
Western needlegrass (*Stipa occidentalis*)
White prairie clover (*Dalea candida*)
Wild rhubarb (*Rumex hymenosepalus*)
Woodland star (*Lithophragma tenella*)
Woollypod milkvetch (*Astragalus purshii*)
Wyoming paintbrush (*Castilleja linariifolia*)
Yellow milkvetch (*Astragalus mollissimus*)
Yellow rabbitbrush (*Chrysothamnus viscidiflorus*)
Yellow salsify (*Tragopogon dubius*)
Zion shooting-star (*Dodecatheon pulchellum* var. *zionense*)

Mammals

Abert's squirrel, or Kaibab squirrel (*Sciurus aberti*)
Allen's big-eared bat (*Idionycteris phyllotis*)
American badger (*Taxidea taxus*)
American beaver (*Castor canadensis*)
American black bear (*Ursus americanus*)
Antelope ground squirrel (*Ammospermophilus* species)
Big brown bat (*Eptesicus fuscus*)
Black-tailed jackrabbit (*Lepus californicus*)
Black-tailed jackrabbit (*Lepus californicus deserticola*)
Bobcat (*Lynx rufus*)
Bushy-tailed woodrat (*Neotoma cinerea*)
California myotis (*Myotis californicus*)
Cliff chipmunk (*Tamias dorsalis*)
Coyote (*Canis latrans*)
Desert cottontail rabbit (*Sylvilagus audubonii*)
Desert shrew (*Notiosorex crawfordi*)
Desert woodrat (*Neotoma lepida*)
Fringed myotis (*Myotis thysanodes*)
Golden-mantled ground squirrel (*Spermophilus lateralis*)
Gray fox (*Urocyon cinereoargenteus*)
Gunnison's prairie dog (*Cynomys gunnisoni*)
Hopi chipmunk (*Neotamias rufus*)
Kit fox (*Vulpes macrotis*)
Least chipmunk (*Neotamias minimus*)
Mexican woodrat (*Neotoma mexicana*)
Mountain lion (*Puma concolor*)
Mule deer (*Odocoileus hemionus*)
North American porcupine (*Erethizon dorsatum*)
Ord's kangaroo rat (*Dipodomys ordii*)
Pallid bat (*Antrozous pallidus*)
Pinyon mouse (*Peromyscus truei*)
Pocket mouse (*Perognathus* spp.)
Porcupine (*Erethizon dorsatum*)
Pronghorn (*Antilocapra americana*)
Raccoon (*Procyon lotor*)
Red fox (*Vulpes vulpes*)
Ringtail (*Bassariscus astutus*)
Rock squirrel (*Otospermophilus variegatus*)

Rocky Mountain bighorn sheep (*Ovis canadensis canadensis*)
Rocky Mountain elk (*Cervus canadensis nelsoni*)
Skunk, or striped skunk (*Mephitis mephitis*)
Tailed weasel (*Mustela frenata*)
Uinta chipmunk (*Neotamias umbrinus*)
Uinta ground squirrel (*Urocitellus armatus*)
Utah prairie dog (*Cynomys parvidens*)
White throated woodrat (*Neotoma albigula*)
White-plustailed antelope squirrel (*Ammospermophilus leucurus*)
Yellow-bellied marmot (*Marmota flaviventris*)

Birds

American dipper (*Cinclus mexicanus*)
American goldfinch (*Spinus tristis*)
American kestrel (*Falco sparverius*)
American robin (*Turdus migratorius*)
Bald eagle (*Haliaeetus leucocephalus*)
Barn swallow (*Hirundo rustica*)
Bewick's wren (*Thryomanes bewickii*)
Black-billed magpie (*Pica hudsonia*)
Black-capped chickadee (*Poecile atricapillus*)
Black-chinned hummingbird (*Archilochus alexandri*)
Black-headed grosbeak (*Pheucticus melanocephalus*)
Black-throated gray warbler (*Setophaga nigrescens*)
Black-throated sparrow (*Amphispiza bilineata*)
Blue-gray gnatcatcher (*Polioptila caerulea*)
Broad-billed hummingbird (*Cynanthus latirostris*)
Broad-tailed hummingbird (*Selasphorus platycercus*)
Broad-winged hawk (*Buteo platypterus*)
Bullock's oriole (*Icterus bullockii*)
Burrowing owl (*Athene cunicularia*)
California condor (*Gymnogyps californianus*)
Calliope hummingbird (*Selasphorus calliope*)
Canyon wren (*Catherpes mexicanus*)
Cedar waxwing (*Bombycilla cedrorum*)
Chipping sparrow (*Spizella passerina*)
Clark's nutcracker (*Nucifraga columbiana*)
Cliff swallow (*Petrochelidon pyrrhonota*)
Common raven (*Corvus corax*)
Cooper's hawk (*Accipiter cooperii*)
Dark-eyed junco (*Junco hyemalis*)
Downy woodpecker (*Picoides pubescens*)
Dusky grouse (*Dendragapus obscurus*)

Evening grosbeak (*Coccothraustes vespertinus*)
Ferruginous hawk (*Buteo regalis*)
Golden eagle (*Aquila chrysaetos*)
Grace's warbler (*Setophaga graciae*)
Greater roadrunner (*Geococcyx californianus*)
Greater sage grouse (*Centrocercus urophasianus*)
Gunnison sage grouse (*Centrocercus minimus*)
Hairy woodpecker (*Picoides villosus*)
Hermit thrush (*Catharus guttatus*)
Horned lark (*Eremophila alpestris*)
House finch (*Haemorhous mexicanus*)
Juniper titmouse (*Baeolophus ridgwayi*)
Lark sparrow (*Chondestes grammacus*)
Mexican spotted owl (*Strix occidentalis lucida*)
Merlin (*Falco columbarius*)
Mountain bluebird (*Sialia currucoides*)
Mountain chickadee (*Poecile gambeli*)
Northern flicker (*Colaptes auratus*)
Northern harrier (*Circus hudsonius*)
Northern pygmy-owl (*Glaucidium gnoma*)
Northern rough-winged hawk (*Stelgidopteryx serripennis*)
Osprey (*Pandion haliaetus*)
Peregrine falcon (*Falco peregrinus*)
Pileated woodpecker (*Dryocopus pileatus*)
Pine siskin (*Spinus pinus*)
Pinyon jay (*Gymnorhinus cyanocephalus*)
Plumbeous vireo (*Vireo plumbeus*)
Prairie falcon (*Falco mexicanus*)
Red-tailed hawk (*Buteo jamaicensis*)
Red-winged blackbird (*Agelaius phoeniceus*)
Rio Grande wild turkey (*Meleagris gallopavo intermedia*)
Rock swift (*Aerodramus fuciphagus*)
Ruby-crowned kinglet (*Regulus calendula*)
Rufous hummingbird (*Selasphorus rufus*)
Sage thrasher (*Oreoscoptes montanus*)
Say's phoebe (*Sayornis saya*)
Scrub jay (*Aphelocoma coerulescens*)
Sharp-shinned hawk (*Accipiter striatus*)
Spotted towhee (*Pipilo maculatus*)
Steller's jay (*Cyanocitta stelleri*)
Swainson's hawk (*Buteo swainsoni*)
Swamp sparrow (*Melospiza georgiana*)
Townsend's solitaire (*Myadestes townsendi*)
Turkey vulture (*Cathartes aura*)
Vaux's swift (*Chaetura vauxi*)
Violet-green swallow (*Tachycineta thalassina*)
Warbling vireo (*Vireo gilvus*)
Western bluebird (*Sialia mexicana*)
Western meadowlark (*Sturnella neglecta*)
Western scrub jay (*Aphelocoma californica*)
Western tanager (*Piranga ludoviciana*)
White-breasted nuthatch (*Sitta carolinensis*)
White-crowned sparrow (*Zonotrichia leucophrys*)

White-throated swift (*Aeronautes saxatalis*)
Wild turkey (*Meleagris gallopavo*)
Williamson's sapsucker (*Sphyrapicus thyroideus*)
Woodhouse's scrub jay (*Aphelocoma woodhouseii*)
Yellow warbler (*Setophaga petechia*)

Fish

Bluehead sucker (*Catostomus discobolus*)
Desert sucker (*Catostomus clarkii*)
Flannelmouth sucker (*Catostomus latipinnis*)
Southern leatherside chub (*Lepidomeda aliciae*)
Speckled dace (*Rhinichthys osculus*)
Virgin spinedace (*Lepidomeda mollispinis*)

Reptiles and Amphibians

Bullsnake (*Pituophis catenifer sayi*)
California king snake (*Lampropeltis californiae*)
Canyon tree frog (*Hyla arenicolor*)
Chihuahuan nightsnake (*Hypsiglena jani*)
Chuckwalla (*Sauromalus ater*)
Common sagebrush lizard (*Sceloporus graciosus*)
Common side-blotched lizard (*Uta stansburiana*)
Desert spiny lizard (*Sceloporus magister*)
Desert striped whipsnake (*Masticophis taeniatus* ssp. *taeniatus*)
Eastern collared lizard (*Crotaphytus collaris*)
Glossy snake (*Arizona elegans*)
Gopher snake (*Pituophis catenifer*)
Great Basin rattlesnake (*Crotalus oreganus lutosus*)
Greater short-horned lizard (*Phrynosoma hernandesi*)
Long-nosed leopard lizard (*Gambelia wislizenii*)
Midget faded rattlesnake (*Crotalus oreganus concolor*)
New Mexico whiptail (*Aspidoscelis neomexicanus*)
Northern plateau lizard (*Sceloporus tristichus*)
Northern whiptail lizard (*Aspidoscelis tigris*)
Pai striped whiptail (*Aspidoscelis pai*)
Plateau fence lizard (*Sceloporus tristichus*)
Plateau striped whiptail (*Aspidoscelis velox*)
Prairie rattlesnake (*Crotalus viridis*)
Short-horned lizard (*Phrynosoma douglasii*)
Side-blotched lizard (*Uta stansburiana*)
Six-lined racerunner (*Aspidoscelis sexlineata*)

Striped whipsnake (*Masticophis taeniatus*)
Terrestrial gartersnake (*Thamnophis elegans*)
Tiger salamander (*Ambystoma tigrinum*)
Tree lizard (*Urosaurus ornatus*)
Western collared lizard (*Crotaphytus collaris*)
Western earless lizard (*Holbrookia maculata*)
Western rattlesnake (*Crotalus viridis*)
Western whiptail (*Aspidoscelis tigris*)
Yellow-bellied racer (*Coluber constrictor flaviventris*)

Insects

Black blister beetle (*Epicauta pennsylvanica*)
Colorado Hairstreak butterfly (*Hypaurotis crysalus*)
Coral Pink Sand Dunes tiger beetle (*Cicindela limbata albissima*)
Harlequin bug (*Murgantia histrionica*)
Sun spider (*Eremobates* spp.)
Tarantula (*Grammostola* spp.)
Velvet ant (*Dasymutilla occidentalis*)
Western tent caterpillar (*Malacosoma californicum*)

Mollusks

Zion snail (*Physella zionis*)

ACKNOWLEDGMENTS

It sure has been a pleasure bringing *Southwest Canyon Country's Best Nature Walks* to life, and I couldn't have done it without the help and support of many colleagues, friends, and family members along the way.

First and foremost, I'd like to thank Ryan Harrington, senior acquisitions editor at Timber Press, for giving me the green light on such a dream project and shepherding it along as it turned from an idea into a reality. Also, Timber editorial assistant Nick Dysinger deserves a lot of credit for keeping the ball rolling from inception to completion. Meanwhile, Timber production editor Matthew Burnett was instrumental in turning a rough-hewn manuscript into the polished opus you are holding in front of you today. This book represents my third title for Timber Press, and I look forward to working on many more moving forward.

Likewise, I couldn't have produced this labor of love without the support of my beloved family. Special thanks go to my parents Ruth and Ken, wife Alex, and kiddos Eliza and Max. (In fact, Ruth, Ken, and Eliza accompanied me on "research" visits to Zion and Bryce, and got to see first-hand how the sausage is made, so to speak.) I'd also like to give a special shout-out to Big Red, my 2003 Volkswagen pop-top Eurovan that made it past 200,000 miles on my research trip to the Southwest for this book—and which just keeps truckin' on.

At the meta level, I'd also like to acknowledge some of the guiding lights who first stirred my interest in Southwest canyon country. The first fan of the flame may have been *Desert Solitaire*, the 1968 memoir by wilderness curmudgeon Edward Abbey, about his time as a park ranger at the idyllic Arches National Monument (before it became a national park) in the late 1950s. This book is a must-read for anyone interested in learning how the region has changed over the last half-century. As I went further down the rabbit hole, I also came to appreciate the dogged work of Stewart Udall, Arizona congressman and Secretary of Interior in the Kennedy and Johnson administrations, who played a key role in the conservation of canyon country. Without the inspired and inspiring work of these two, among others, there might not be any national parks to visit in the Southwest.

PHOTO AND ILLUSTRATION CREDITS

All photographs by the author, except for the following:

Alamy
Danita Delimont Creative, 174

Dreamstime
Cjchiker, 245
Danler, Lake Powell illustration
Rainer Lesniewski, Grand Canyon illustration
Studiobarcelona, 163

iStock
Brent_1, 123 (left)
J Curtis, 185 (bottom left)
Jamesvancouver, 176
viavado, 180
Wolfgang Gafriller, 162

Flickr
Loving Wanderer 12, 157

CC BY 2.0
NPS/Michael Quinn, 154

Shutterstock
Agami Photo Agency, 156
Anatoliy Lukich, 81 (bottom)
escap, 160
Frank Fichtmueller, 94 (bottom right)
Gaelyn Olmsted, 170
James Marvin Phelps, 49 (top)
Morphart Creation, prickly pear and Rocky Mountain pine illustrations
Stephen Moehle, 178–179
Thomas BLANK, 158

Wikimedia
CC BY 4.0
Claytondodge9, 172–173

INDEX

RODDY SCHEER is a journalist and photographer specializing in environmental issues, the outdoors, and travel. When he is not out in the field taking pictures, Roddy produces EarthTalk, a weekly environmental Q&A column syndicated to more than 1000 news outlets reaching more than 6 million readers. He has served as a regular contributor to *E-The Environmental Magazine*, *Seattle Magazine*, *Northwest Travel*, *American Photo*, *PhotoMedia*, *Wildflower*, and others. His books include *Oregon and Washington's Roadside Ecology* and *Yellowstone and Grand Teton's Best Nature Walks*. He is a three-time Society of Professional Journalists "Excellence in Journalism" winner.